The Genius of 10th St.

Robert Roth

Published by And Then Press, 2026.

THE GENIUS OF 10TH ST.

First edition. January 1, 2026.

ISBN: 979-8991833882

Written by Robert Roth.

Table of Contents

Dedicated to the memory of Víctor Asencio whose powerful imagination and moral guidance I still carry with me in these times of both horror and resistance.

About twenty years ago Michael Kranish who was a manager at a public housing project in NYC one night saw a security guard recently here from Puerto Rico sitting in his security booth reading my uncle Sandor Voros's book *American Commissar*. The book is about my uncle fighting in Spain during the Spanish Civil War. It was published in the mid 1950s. There might be only 10 copies of the book left in the world. Somehow he got hold of one of them. And there he was 60 years later reading my long dead uncle's long out of print book. And on top of that meeting a good friend of the author's nephew.

To have just one person way in the future stumble onto something I wrote and get absorbed in it, argue with it, spin out with it, do whatever they will do with it, is beyond thrilling. Maybe they'll search for other things I have written, or use it as a key to a universe way in the past. Embark on an effort to discover something about the world I inhabited and people I knew. What if they follow the clues or information or evidence to wherever they lead. What might they find?

The thoughts, discoveries, mis-discoveries and interpretations of what they do find will be presented in italics throughout the book.

I think that is a brilliant idea.

"I'm glad you like it."

"I wish I had thought of it myself."

There are Many of Us

There are so many people with the same name as me. People whose politics, whose sensibilities at least from afar or maybe even up close are very similar to mine. All in fact have done impressive things in their lives.

The subtle distinctions I make, the choosing of words to express my deepest thoughts/feelings/political perspectives seem totally useless in distinguishing me from the others.

Still there are things I sometimes seriously disagree with, sometimes there are things I know nothing about. And often enough things are said in ways I wish I was the one who had said them. Particularly if sometime way in the future I am going to get credit for it.

How will those differences be reconciled?

Robert said one thing here. Another thing there. He doesn't even acknowledge that he is doing it.

Robert Roth author. As a working-class queer nerd and author, **Roth** uses his writing to challenge the status quo and question the capitalist patriarchy.

Robert Roth (artist) paints idyllic visions of landscapes seen from a distance. Roth's atmospheric works, influenced by Modern luminaries ranging from...

Robert Roth (born 1950) was an active member in the anti-war, anti-racism and anti-imperialism movements of the 1960s and 70s, and key member of the Students for a Democratic Society (SDS) political movement in the Columbia University Chapter in New York, where he eventually presided. Later, as a member of the Weatherman/Weather Underground Organization he used militant tactics to oppose the Vietnam War and racism. After the war ended, Roth surfaced from his underground status and has been involved in a variety of social causes to this day.

I first learned about this Robert Roth when a woman I met at a movie screening called me and pretty early on in the conversation told me she once had an affair with him. And while not being in the grip of a powerful and rare fetish, she did find the thought intriguing of maybe us having an affair also.

Often after seeing my name on a mailing list or a petition, I would get emails, phone calls and letters from people who thought I was him. Talking about some shared experience from the past. I would have to tell them that it wasn't me.

And just a couple of years ago a new neighbor looked me up and was so impressed with what she read that no matter what I said I couldn't convince her that he wasn't me.

Robert Roth (born 1966) is a songwriter, vocalist and guitarist of 1990s Sub Pop and Capitol Records band Truly. He is still touring today.

And then there was **Robert Roth** gay movie critic, as opposed to the novelist, who died a number of years ago. I think he may have also started a film magazine in Chicago.

And what about the Robert Roth who wrote an eloquent letter to the NY Post furious at George H.W. Bush for calling someone retarded. He wrote about his two children who had Down syndrome and the wounding ignorance that slurs like that have as well as what they reveal about the person using them.

Robert had at least two children. I see he got acknowledgments in landmark books on disability. Yes. It is very likely he wrote the letter. As far as I know, he *didn't write about his children anywhere else. That doesn't mean it is not true.* He *has a brother who he rarely mentions also. But I did find a manuscript of scattered typed sheets where he wrote a lot about him.*

Then there was the **Robert Roth** who made an anti-war movie. He fought in Vietnam.

Now it is possible some of these Robert Roths are actually the same person. What do I know?

There was also a person whose name was close to mine who wrote a letter to Seven Days, the radical weekly not the sleek trendy weekly of a few years later, that a number of friends—yes friends—complimented me on.

And then there was the **Robert Roth** fighting for the preservation of landmark buildings on the upper west side of Manhattan. Why not?

Mobilizing support he used all his political organizing skills to convince people who thought there were more pressing problems that it wasn't a question of either/or. It was important as a way to resist the uglification of the city and the desire to erase history and that the huge power of the real estate industry had to be prevented from imposing its will whenever, wherever it pleased. He learned the history of architecture in New York. He became an expert on the social political economic forces at play when the buildings were built. He was very well versed in housing law. All this while touring the world with his band, raising at least two children. He was continually on the front lines of social activism, and while there is no recorded evidence it was rumored that he was the last person to swim the English Channel before it became a stretch of hard dry dirt.

And before I forget there was an article in New York magazine that a Robert Roth and Arnold Socher opened up a club in lower Manhattan featuring drag performers.

That has to be them. Arnie's name is a little off in the spelling. It should be Sachar. But mistakes like that happened all the time.

It was mind blowing to stumble across this article. Arnie and I did so much together. We wrote poetry, short stories, public statements and public petitions where we had to gather signatures of as many people as we could. Our politics roughly, anarchist, pacifist, sex radical. We organized discussion groups, writing groups, sometimes gatherings to discuss a particular issue. We started And Then together with Shelley

Haven and Marguerite Bunyan. So in some alternative universe we might have opened up a drag club. Again just reading the article some people might just assume it was us. In addition Arnie one time heard both our fathers discussing what kind of business they could set us up in. They were worried about our future. He said it was both funny and moving hearing them trying to grasp who we were and trying to figure if there was anything at all that could be done.

One time I did meet a Swiss banker at the 60th wedding anniversary of my aunt and uncle and spoke to him for about a half hour discussing the finances of the magazine and what it took for us to break even. "If lovers or friends or family members of the contributors buy copies that is a big plus." [Sadly since writing this I learned that after my uncle and aunt died there was a bitter falling out between him and my cousin, their granddaughter, which clearly diminishes the memory of this exchange.]

Dead Friend Press

Stephanie's novel 40% done.

Muriel's book about her therapist crossing basic sexual boundaries 97% done.

Shulamith's novel 100% done.

Karen's memoir one chapter short of being done (there are extensive notes of what she might have included in the section).

My mother's dissertation 100% done.

A writer I greatly admired and was friendly with died and left boxes and boxes of notebooks filled with descriptions of people, interactions of people in various circumstances, descriptions of nature and small town life. Powerful thoughtful descriptions infused with the full power of his genius. His two literary executors poured through them and selected sections and put them together into a book. Both were fine writers and though half a generation younger shared a similar sensibility. But even though all the words were entirely his, the book itself, how these sections interacted with each other was entirely theirs. It was unsettling. You had absolutely no idea how he might have used each of those sections in some larger work. In the way the sections were arranged, the book seemed much more politically and culturally conservative than any other work of his I had ever read. The executors were very close friends of his. So maybe they remained faithful to how he saw the world at that time.

I hope not.

One time I read an article by a friend of mine that appeared in Ms. She and I had some political differences over the years. But in the article those differences were taken way beyond anything I had read from her before. I saw her later that week and she was livid. They had changed her ending without telling her. She was very embarrassed and distraught that people would think she would say those things.

I ran into another friend sometime later who said *The Nation* just published an article under her name where they changed every word of it.

In the first issue of *And Then* Volume One, 1987 we published a conversation between Gary Sheinfeld and James Baldwin.

> Baldwin: Giovani's Room was one of the most troubling I've written. You know I was warned not to publish it.... I'm a Negro writer and I can't afford to alienate an audience...they told me. I don't think any artist can be told who his audience is or what to write. I believe you had a similar problem, with your short story, about a black child on the subway.
>
> Sheinfeld: I think so. Yes at Columbia the editors of this journal wanted to publish it, but they said it was a racist story, because a white man is able to calm a black child while her mother remains helpless. They wanted to change a few key words. I asked them not to, I'd rather they not publish the story. They assured me they wouldn't change a word. They published it after changing "white" to "withered."
>
> Baldwin: It was a very beautiful story, very bitter, but very beautiful.

Now my uncle told me that Esquire wanted to change the ending of a short story he wrote. He told them he wouldn't. So they didn't publish the story. He felt he made a grave error. No other opportunity of that magnitude came his way again.

So my way-in-the-future biographer sleuth soulmate friend collaborator can't be sure that whatever appeared under my name, assuming it was actually me, really was what I had intended. Also will they have to track down these unpublished works of friends of mine.

And follow wherever they lead. Traces of me might be found in at least some of them.

We published the original version of Gary's story in And Then Volume 2, 1989.

Acknowledgments

One time in the 1970s a woman came over to me and said I can't read a book about feminism without seeing your name in the acknowledgments. This has been true of many other subjects as well. Jazz, opera, Eastern Europe, cook books, even real estate to name a very few. Books, articles, dissertations, an occasional footnote, being mentioned in the program of concerts and plays. Called out from the stage by a singer in between songs. Is he a critic, does he work for a record label, a producer, a musician, a song writer, a family member, a former lover? There are works that I feel particularity attached to. And then there are poems and prose pieces and music pieces dedicated to me over the years. I feel very appreciative and grateful and deeply moved when that happens. But still it might not be so apparent to someone looking back from the future as to the "why" of some of those acknowledgments.

As the lights went on in the darkened theater, my name was the last to appear in a long list of credits that rolled across the screen of When Two Worlds Collide, a documentary about the struggle over resources in the Peruvian Amazon. The credits disappeared in the Netflix version, eliminating crucial primary source material. Basically my role was to put the filmmakers up in my apartment when they came to New York. I also accompanied them to Chinatown where they bought film equipment from the back of a van.

How Reputations are Formed

My friend Marvin Schwartz was the official photographer for the Calder exhibit at the Museum of Modern Art. The animal sculptures for the mobiles to be assembled were all inside a roped off area. Marvin stepped over the rope and started combing the hair of one of the lions.

A higher up in the museum, worried that he would damage the lion, started racing toward him waving her arms frantically yelling for him to stop.

A friend of Marvin who worked there raised his hand and said, "But Marvin is a genius." She stopped in her tracks and said, Oh!"

And that, according to Marvin, is how he became a genius.

*

Roth's understanding of the cultural, political and economic forces in Peru was legendary.

A friend was doing a dissertation on the political economy of Peru, very detailed very technical work. Different from the more accessible, incisive essays she wrote for various leftwing journals. As we were putting together the first issue of And Then, I asked her if she could write an essay about the clashing economic forces in Peru. Instead she wrote a magnificent poem about Peru and the infliction of economic pain by powerful forces there to plunder the country. One great thing in doing the magazine is that I always have to let go of whatever preconceived idea I have about what the person will do. Usually it does take a couple of days to adjust. And then, Wow!

I also remember my friend once did a phone interview with Noam Chomsky. They just couldn't click on anything. Noam said, Let's try again tomorrow. And they did. And it went extremely well.

In any case, the dissertation was being written in very technical language. At one point she got totally stuck, I suggested that each month she send me something that she had written, "It will give you a goal, something to shoot for. I won't understand a word but so what."

So each month she sent me a number of pages she had written. And I was right. I couldn't understand one word. Still I read everything she sent. One month she sent me something that somehow made less sense than everything else that made no sense to me. With great hesitation I wrote back and told her that maybe there was something off about that section. Being an exceptionally warm, generous and considerate person, she tried to be as nice about it as possible. Reminding me that my role basically was to be someone to send something to each month to motivate her to keep her on track and to mark her progress. That she very much appreciated what I was doing but there were no expectations beyond that. I loved her even more than before for the care she took in telling me that.

Three days later she called and apologized, telling me that her dissertation advisors told her that section was a total mess.

Later she submitted an article to a journal where an outside reader wrote a totally ridiculous nitpicking critique. I said why don't we turn this into a poem. And we took the words from the critique and arranged them into a poem. We called it Reader's Comments. It was published in a Socialist newspaper. Previously we had submitted it to Monthly Review. Paul Sweezy, one of the most important Marxian economists of the 20th Century who was both founder and editor of Monthly Review wrote back an absolutely gracious, apologetic rejection letter saying how much he liked our poem but the Review didn't publish poetry. It was such a high being personally rejected by him in this way.

Still as rejection letters go it was a distant second compared to the one another friend once received. When her short story was rejected by a very prestigious literary journal, the editor wrote, "Sorry. I just don't get it." In a handwritten note underneath, the woman working as his secretary added, "But I do."

In addition to being an adviser for a major documentary and the go to guy when it came to understanding the Peruvian economy, there was his life long friendship and collaboration with Fredy Roncalla, Peruvian writer, poet, musician, literary critic, political analyst that was crucial to the forming of his deep grasp of the subtleties and intricacies and beauties of Peruvian culture. Fredy and Robert wrote poetry together and essays. They would meet every Sunday before the flea market opened where Fredy would sell his jewelry. While they often conversed just with each other, people would gather nearby and try to overhear their conversation. So immersed were they in conversation they barely noticed other people being there. Even though the conversations moved seamlessly back and forth through Quechua, Spanish and English, what they were saying could immediately be understood by anyone who just spoke any one of those languages. It was a vivid example for a discipline started a couple of decades later by someone overhearing them and then using them as the original model to build a whole theory around. It is the study of how through facial expressions, intonations of the voice and an overflowing humanity and intimacy, "understanding" in its rawest and most authentic form, can break free from the confines imposed by spoken language.

There was immediate pushback from poets who knew them both and who thought to reduce them into being examples for a new academic discipline was a way to neutralize the actual expansive power of the words themselves.

No one knows how Robert at 105 or Fredy at 95, who were known to still meet regularly, felt about any of it.

Poet, composer, librettist, economist, cultural critic, map maker, all around troubleshooter

Two super close friends of mine who were working on an opera had a bitter falling out. They wanted to complete the opera but because each had taken an order of protection out against the other, they couldn't be in the same room together. I was asked to be the go between.

One would say, "You go tell her that..." I would answer, "I can't 'you go tell her that.' There must be a better way to say it." Only to have the other person then say, "You go tell him that..." "I can't 'you go tell him that'...!'"

I also received a phone call from an entertainment lawyer who was beside herself about what to do. And so on and so forth until the opera was completed.

And what an opera it was! And just for the record they later made peace and went on to do other magnificent things together.

There was a reading of the opera in the huge loft of the director. Instruments from the 13th century to the present in one section, posters on the wall from hit shows he had directed on other walls. In the program there was a special mention of how indispensable I was to the completion of the opera.

Afterward I was approached by a number of people. They asked if in some way I helped with the libretto. Or just assuming that I must have some vast knowledge of music did I help get over any rough spots in the composing of the music.

So if that program is ever discovered in the directors papers or written about in the biographies of the composer and/or the librettist, or even somehow salvaged from wherever it is in my apartment, it will provide further evidence of my multiple talents as a writer and musician. While my ability as a world class mediator will simply get lost in the shuffle.

*

Just as I was completing this section, I received Ahmed Abdullah's memoir *A Strange Celestial Road: My Time in the Sun Ra Arkestra*. In the introduction he described a conversation we had In Prospect Park in 1997 that helped start him on creating this historic work. It felt so good to read. He and his life partner the oh so brilliant poet and singer Monique Ngozi Nri have been a constant source of validation over the decades.

What I haven't written about here is how much I like writing acknowledgments myself.

Often when I write acknowledgments I get swept away with pleasure in celebrating people who are vital to my life. If these acknowledgments survive into the future they will provide a treasure trove of clues for My Looking Back into the Past (my present) Companion. They will provide a sense of the people I knew, the environments I was part of. The joys, the terrors, the ferment, the tragedies, the magic and richness of sharing this time on earth with all these wondrous people I love beyond measure.

Pen Names, Pseudonyms, New Names, Different Names

Doris Lessing wrote two short novels under the name Jane Somers to see how people would respond to her work not knowing it was her who had written them. It was also done to highlight the difficulties of unknown writers getting their work published. A respected publishing house rejected the novel out of hand. A small publisher finally published it. It received a couple of short reviews that were low key in their praise. Of course when it was revealed who wrote them all that changed.

Both novels were released as a paperback called "*The Diary of a Good Neighbor*." I got a copy of it as a present. Many years later the Living Theatre did an adaptation of one of the novels. The play was called *Maudie and Jane*. Judith Molina was breathtaking as the lead character.

*

One time in my early 30s I was more or less just staring through the window of the New Yorker Bookstore not focusing on anything in particular when Stanley Aronowitz, radical social critic, author of many books and articles, and non stop political organizer came to stand next to me. He pointed to a book and asked if I knew who the author was. I said I didn't. He then told me it was a pseudonym that Murray Bookchin the great anarchist theorist used at some point in the past, quickly adding that he thought it was cowardly of Bookchin and anyone else not to write under their own name. He sounded totally ridiculous.

Without even thinking I blurted out. "Well people have their reasons. In fact I've written books under a different name that you use in your courses." Which was totally untrue.

Stanley was one of the creators of The Free Association, a radical libertarian socialist/anarchist school. He was in his early 40s. He had a huge personality. A mix of insecurity, massive ego, profound commitments, genuine accomplishments, warmth and a compulsive need to assert his brilliance and importance.

From treating me like an "equal" he was now very unsure and clearly nervous about where I fell in his hierarchy of importance.

"Robert, Do you write popular best sellers?"

"No, radical social criticism. Like I said, you are using my books in your courses."

He grew more nervous.

"You can tell me. I promise I won't tell anyone."

"I've said too much already," I replied, a bit guilty that I was carrying it too far, but still locked into it.

"Really. You can tell me. I won't tell anyone."

"Forget I said anything. I was just joking."

A few days later Joyce Johnson, the writer and editor, who organized a writers group I was part of, came over to me at the The Free Association. With a big conspiratorial smile on her face she whispered that Stanley had come over to her apartment after our exchange and asked her who I really was.

She said she answered, "I'm sworn to secrecy."

Now I'm not one to talk. A scene for a movie was being filmed in a long unoccupied bar on the corner of my block. I stood behind a police barricade watching the filming when an extremely friendly black man his shoulder warmly leaning into mine started talking to me. He was straight out fun and we just got into a totally riotous back and forth. We were talking and laughing when suddenly it dawned on me that it was Richard Pryor. My voice cracked in mid sentence. I tried to continue as if nothing was different. Fortunately for me he had to go back to work.

"Nice talking to you, man."

"Nice talking to you too."

A number of years after my conversation with Stanley in front of the bookstore, while attending an anarchist conference in the early 1980s in Montreal, I showed Murray Bookchin a copy of a magazine where my short story *In the Audience* had recently been published. It was the first story of mine published since college.

It was a long short story. It had the feel of a novella, even a novel. It was about people who inhabited an alternative universe of radicals, who had one foot in and one foot out of the mainstream world that they were trying to change, overthrow and yet find a place in. The ways also they had internalized the values of the dominant culture and how the impact of those values seriously undermined the types of transformations they, with great imagination and courage, were devoting their lives to achieving.

As soon as Murray took the magazine from me his eyes lit up. A big smile crossed his face. He saw that Raymond Aron had an essay in it and without even the faintest acknowledgment or congratulations turned immediately to Aron's essay. On top of it he wanted me to share in his delight. Those tiny slights, these tiny hurts, in this case more an expression of his massive self-absorption than any desire to diminish me, though in this case I wasn't even present enough to be diminished, can, at least by me, be quickly rationalized away, overly understood and easily buried. Only to unexpectedly surface like now many, many decades later.

*

Early in her career, the brilliant Argentine pianist Arminda Canteros developed a huge reputation as a classical musician. But unknown to most people she was also an extraordinary tango player. At the time it was considered unseemly for a woman to play the tango. It was considered too bold, too sexually assertive. Somehow a radio station hired her to have her own show where she would play the tango. But they insisted she assume a male persona whose name would be Jacinto. People went crazy over Jacinto and during the 1930s and 40s, he developed an avid following. To keep the ruse going they created a whole ongoing story about his life. For example the publicist from the station would feed juicy gossip items to the local tabloids. *Last weekend Jacinto and a beautiful (unnamed) starlet were sighted at a romantic hide away by the ocean.*

Eventually the stigma of women playing the tango lifted and Arminda would give full concerts performing as herself. Over the years she would tour the world sometimes doing classical music concerts, other times concerts where she only played the tango. Once in New York after a tango concert, an older man came up to her and said it was the most beautiful tango he had heard since listening to someone named Jacinto play the tango on the radio a long long time ago.

I went to a concert of Bennet Lerner who had once been a student of hers. It was through him I had met Arminda who was also at the concert. The concert was in the small theatre inside a piano store. After the recital there was a reception in an upstairs showroom filled with pianos. Bennett was on the far end of the room when he heard one note coming way from the other end. Arminda had hit just one key on one of the pianos. As if almost connected by an invisible string, you could actually see Bennett's ears perk up as he spun around searching, smiling, instantly knowing who had played the note and where it had come from.

*

My uncle keeps popping up in this piece. I sent my cousin Jos Kraay, Sandor's daughter, the first few pages of Genius of 10th St. where I write about her father. She sent me this email in reply.

Thank you Robert, what is a name. When my father Sandor as the last of the family went from Hungry to Amerika, he was asked his name. He thought it would be better to not give up his Hungarian name, Voros,

Voros was a translation of red from Russian, so he translated and as red, he meant Roth, but they understood Wrought, therefore his name is different from the rest but sounds the same. When Sandor was here in Amsterdam in 1966, we went to the big synagogue at the Waterloopplein, Sandor said to the woman who was in the entrance that he was not a jew at all, she laughed and said you are an Askenace.

My uncle used two names. Alex Wrought in his daily life and Sandor Voros in his creative public life. People keep asking me if I have an uncle Philip. I do. But not the Philip they are asking about. My uncle Philip was pretty spectacular in his own right. His name was Philip Voros. He toured the country as a mind reader. Also held private mind reading sessions at rich people's homes. He had a photographic memory and developed a recipe for diet bread. A bread company stole his recipe. I saw an item in the newspaper that he won a suit against the company and was awarded damages. Not exactly a fortune, but still something.

When I was in the first grade we went around the room to introduce ourselves. I said I was Robert Roth (pronouncing it as Wrought) The teacher said, No it's "Roth." I said it was "Wrought." I was furious. I went home all upset and told my father they said my name is Roth. I told them it was Wrought. He said they're right it is Wrought. He tried to pronounce "th "and just couldn't. Even now I have a slight moment of hesitation and discomfort when I have to say my last name.

My father, Irving Roth, who came here from Hungary as a kid was never fully comfortable in any language. He spoke Hungarian, English and a bit of Yiddish.

Twice I wrote a letter to the editor using the name Laszlo Voros, Laszlo being my middle name, my mother's "maiden" name. I felt a sense of freedom to write something I thought, without the need to add a 10th qualification to what I was saying. I also named a character in a short story Robert Laszlo. My father got a particular kick out seeing a character who clearly wasn't based on me with that name.

As for Jos. Her mother met my uncle in Spain. She had volunteered as a nurse in the fight against Franco. She and my uncle had an affair there and Jos was conceived. With the defeat of the International Brigade her mother went back to The Netherlands and my uncle came back here. Fast forward. For reasons too complex to go into here, Jos and Sandor met for the first time when Jos was in her late 20s. I knew nothing of her existence until I was in Amsterdam in 1967 where my aunt Gladys was also visiting. I went to see Gladys in her hotel room and with maybe only five minutes of a heads up, in strides this woman dressed in black leather, all filled with attitude, passion, warmth and having something to say about everything. In short, looking and sounding like all the people on my father's side of the family. She is now in her mid 80s. Five books could be written about the astounding life she has lived.

*

Many people have written pieces for And Then using a variety of names, sometimes writing under different names in the same issue. I never ever reveal who wrote what except with their permission, even with a co-editor. In issue two we published a couple wrenching, jumping with energy, personal letters to ex lovers written under different names. At some point one of the writers, someone pretty well known, became very frustrated that people didn't know it was them that had written the letter. So they said I could reveal it if it came up. The person they had written the letter to originally had made a number of other lovers miserable in the same ways. Once I could reveal who wrote the letter, I sold a bunch of issues to those who had waited by the phone for the call that never came.

*

I invited my friend Shulamith Firestone into a discussion group. She was withdrawing from public life and really didn't want to be recognized during that period in time. She agreed but only if I introduced her as Kathy and not tell anyone who she was. I agreed. It was not a great thing to agree to. At the end of the day it was worth it. Because our friendship blossomed. But I would never do it again except if someone was really in trouble. Because you are constantly making up things on the run, misdirecting, deceiving. It became very unpleasant.

One time someone in the group brought up her book The Dialectic of Sex. As the person was about to say something, the conversation shifted direction. Shulamith laughed and later said that that would have been the only time she would have heard a totally honest response to her book from someone who didn't know they were speaking to her.

Over the years Shulamith used various versions of her name. You can identify each distinct period of her life as well as when any one of us met her by what name of hers we use. As well as what name we use when writing about her.

*

It was rumored that Roth wrote many books under a whole series of different names. He was very prolific. Each name opened up a whole wide avenue for expression. Before computers James Baldwin, the iconic mid to late 20th century Black author had typewriters (a popular writing instrument of that period) in different parts of his house in Southern France, each with a piece of paper from a different book he was working on.

But in Robert's case no one really knows. He was very secretive about it. In a surviving oral history recording a friend of Ann Snitow (Ann is credited with being instrumental in forming what was known as the second wave of the feminist movement), said Ann had introduced her to Robert whom she called a "major figure in the downtown art scene." It was said by many others that his endorsement of an event would guarantee a huge turnout.

Asked about Ann's description of him, Robert at the time replied that he didn't even know what the downtown art scene was. But that he went straight home and wrote a poem.

Roth was protective of these multiple creative identities. He would never acknowledge that any of them were him. Or maybe in fact all those disputed identities were really other people and not him. As a biographer, historian and sleuth I am torn whether I am justified in revealing identities he kept protected. A kind of outing that has no real purpose. What are my responsibilities to him/they and what is it to history. Compounding it all, I am far from certain who wrote anything other than what has survived. Things written under his name are in the Aronowitz Pavilion where relics from the ancient moderns are stored. So even speculating out loud about authorship of works attributed to others creates doubt. Even if disproved, once that doubt is there, it remains there forever.

One thing I plan to discuss though are unattributed social political psychological categories he created as well as aphorisms he wrote without signing his name to them, that have become part of the language. I will trace them back to him and discuss their original meanings and discuss how those meanings have changed and evolved over time.

Part two or multipage footnote

"Who are you favorite writers?"

"Margaret, Amir, Brian, Tania, Marlene, Gilbert."

No. I mean who are your favorite writers?"

"I just told you. Tania, Amir, Margaret, Gabbie, Brian, Marlene, Gilbert. Oh I forgot to include Luisa."

"I mean who are your favorite writers?"

"And you too of course."

*

I delivered newspapers for close to 30 years. For a few of those years I delivered the Poetry Calendar to various locations throughout the city. Hundreds of events were listed. Within the pages of the calendar no event was privileged over any other. Unlike most of the other things we delivered this felt like something more than just a job. My boss was Donald Lev, who with Enid Dame, was co-editor of Home Planet News. Both Donald and Enid were almost mythic presences on the alternative poetry scene. For him delivering the Calendar was part of his poetic calling. For me it was still a job. But a job with emotional benefits. HPN, Central Park, Socialist Review, Socialism and Democracy and The Sun were older siblings of And Then. Our magazine reflected different aspects of each. Working with Donald we had endless discussions in the van, a kind of constant cross fertilization of our two publications.

In the calendar no event or any particular writer was treated as more important than any other. So at least inside its pages everyone was treated equally. The poetry calendar was sold and taken over by very politically astute, culturally aware editors whose entrepreneurial energy mixed with insurgent cultural awareness would, in their minds, merge seamlessly with the most dynamic forces inside the poetry scene. In this new vision of things certain events and writers were highlighted. Who could object? The cutting edge writers to be featured were part of something vital. And the new poetry calendar was going to reflect that vitality, to amplify it. In the very first issue there was a beautiful photo of a friend of mine on the cover. Along with a very warm profile of her which included an interview about her life and work. It was a strange feeling. My dear friend through no fault of her own, an active symbol of my [am not sure what word to use]. And here I am distributing her all over the city. Which under normal circumstances would be downright thrilling. It was ironic and a bit comical, but still genuinely unsettling. In what was started as a service to a community where multi hierarchies of talent, status, location, power, money, lack of money and consciousness often felt intractable, the calendar reflected the part of that world filled with yearning, respect and far reaching artistic ferment. The new calendar pretty much was designed to become an organ of all the stratifications inside the poetry world or probably more accurately in the semi alternative, semi insurgent version of it.

All this was clashing inside me as I was carrying a bundle of the calendars to Poetry House when it was still located in a small office in SoHo. Convincing myself that I was less upset than I was, rather than waiting until I could put the bundle on a table to cut the plastic straps binding it, I took out my box cutter and tried to cut it open while walking. The blade slipped and I badly sliced a couple of my fingers. Back in the van, I wrapped my fingers with a page from one of the newspapers we were delivering to absorb the blood and try to slow down the bleeding. We went straight to a clinic where I got my fingers stitched up.

When Arnie Sachar and I started discussing doing And Then we wanted it to be as open as possible. The age range over the years has been 5 to people in their 90s. A mix of people who saw themselves as writers and artists and people who didn't. It could be someone who hadn't written since junior high school and some who weren't yet old enough to be in kindergarten. And it would include a whole range of people coming from different backgrounds different cultures. People with widely different experiences. We decided early on not to have readers notes except where it was crucial to what was being written about. So at least inside the pages of the magazine the pieces and contributors were all equal. Marguerite Bunyan and Shelley Haven who started the magazine with us, who worked on the design over the years tried as much as possible not to have one piece privileged over any other. Nothing was considered or treated as a filler.

While doing the first issue of And Then I asked my friend Gary Scheinfeld, a writer and close friend of James Baldwin if he thought Baldwin would agree to interview Gary for the magazine. I thought it would be an interesting reversal. I very definitely didn't want it the other way around. It started out as the interview we envisioned and quickly evolved into this powerful conversation between two close friends who loved and admired each other deeply. Sadly the conversation chronicled [James Baldwin's, Baldwin's, Jimmy's] last day alive in the United States. The piece ended as he was about to board a plane back to France where he died a few months later.

Kate Millet also agreed to contribute an art work. How did this come about? I was going with a friend to an exhibit of hers. The Loony Bin Trip was about her experiences in the mental hospital. On the way there my friend had just given me a copy of a publication he was working on. I said why don't you wait, maybe you would like to give a copy to her. He said he is not into that type of thing and I should just keep it. We were in the room for maybe thirty seconds when he grabbed the magazine out of my hands and ran to give her the copy. The exhibition was of Kate's drawings. I thought maybe she would give us one for the magazine. I spoke to my friend to try and get up the nerve. He said he would ask her and he did. And she agreed. He then said to me, maybe she could do the cover. Why the fuck are you suggesting that when you know Shelley is doing the cover. I was really angry. But there is where the temptation and the corruption begins. Two world famous artists appearing in the very first issue. And one doing the cover.

What are you guided by, a silly sense of loyalty? Big things can happen here. And of course it wasn't just loyalty to Shelley that I would be betraying but also the deep sense of exhilaration and satisfaction that I got from working with her. And the spectacular creation she would come up with for the cover.

Fortunately and unfortunately because of certain questions of logistics things fell through with Kate and the drawing. I pretty much let it slide. I was in fact more relieved than disappointed.

Here were two people, public figures, who politically and spiritually were as close to us as could be. We had some personal connection to each. In that sense it was organic and continuous to how we took in the world. Still to have two world famous artists in the first issue would have very possibly killed something vital to its emerging essence.

Recognizable names (just because someone was well known didn't mean that they wouldn't be included) in a sense helps everyone else in the magazine. It draws attention to the magazine and everyone in it. But the down side and it is a very serious downside, is that a very famous public person no matter how you might want to get around it will create the lens though which the magazine will be seen. And the stratification in the outside world will reproduce itself almost immediately in how most people will take in the other work. As well as how the magazine itself will be defined.

*

Recently, I finished reading Ahmed Abdullah's memoir *A Strange Celestial Road: My Time in the Sun Ra Arkestra*.

In addition to being an extraordinary musician and band leader (and friend), Ahmed is a vivid story teller. Reading the book you actually hear the "music of the spirit" pulling you along as you keep turning the pages.

The book is one of celebration, yearning; a deep exploration of creativity, pain. Connection. Resistance.

Profound social and cultural analysis is laced throughout. Oppression, neglect and brutality in the overt and more subtle forms are looked at, then looked at again. He describes and reacts to the devastating fault lines in the society as well as the serious fault lines that [exist, are created] in the responses to it.

It is a story of his life beginning at a young age, but also of Sun Ra's vast, remarkable life, and Ahmed's complicated, at times tense relationship with him. There are many crucial historic and personal insights about Ahmed's life in the Arkestra. His own years as a musician performing with it. The book also brings to life the musician driven Loft Movement of the 70s. Insurgent, communal and forging an alternative vibrant music [scene, community]. The Loft Movement grew as a response to forces of repression and oppression and marginalization. We see people immersed in a culture of intense ongoing creativity. We see the tragedies that can unfold. The tensions, the cruelties, the intense disconnectedness as well as the profound life affirming creativity of the musicians. The strains and pains pulling at them. The enormous love binding them together.

These dynamics are important to look at and understand. But what also is looked at with extreme sensitivity is how new and far reaching insights when applied to real people in real situations can curdle and become dehumanizing and one dimensional. Insights hardening into truism can at times be comical, absurd but also deeply hurtful if not outright destructive.

One particular scene keeps playing itself out in my head. There was an all black music venue where whites were excluded. It was presented and thought of by the people running it as an autonomous liberated space, space free of the intrinsic racist dynamics that would automatically be set in motion even if the most decent white person would be there. One night a number of groups were scheduled to perform. A musician came with his white [girlfriend, partner, woman]. The man at the door said the woman couldn't come in. He was somewhat uncomfortable doing it, glancing in her direction saying no disrespect intended. The musician was indignant. Particularly so since no one told him about the policy beforehand. Back and forth like this. The woman spoken about in the third person, treated more like an object of contention than a person, finally expressed her own bewilderment and anger. Then a parting shot of anger from the musician as they left.

If she had come into the venue, the dynamics inside would change instantly. Keeping her out, a real person not an abstraction, intrinsically changed the dynamics inside also. And winds up being written about in a book 50 years later.

Discussed briefly but pointedly in Salim Washington's Forward, and alluded to inside the book itself, without Salim or Ahmed fully going into the whys of it, the sexual, romantic relationships between white women and black men is spoken about as a particularly complex and fraught one.

Inside the venue that night groups performing would create beautiful music together. The venue and others like it were in significant and real ways liberated territory. Where racism and humiliation and oppression [dissolves, melts away, is transformed]. But also at the time except maybe for occasional dancers and/or singers, transcendent in their otherworldly/this worldly brilliance, black women for the most part, if at all, were not performing with any of the groups. Instruments like the trumpet or the saxophone were played exclusively by men. Invisibility, one of the most powerful tools of oppression, one that the male musicians knew all too well and had resisted with great courage and imagination, was being used against women musicians without giving it a second thought. Except where it was willfully and very consciously done.

"Certainly, [Sun Ra's] views on women were stringent, whether they were Black or white. Sometimes he'd say that women interfered with the creative process, so much so that he didn't encourage females to attend rehearsals. But then he'd make exceptions. June, for example, was one woman who was regularly allowed to be in on rehearsals. She seemed to transcend every one of Sunny's dictums and helped to create his persona—the enigma wrapped in a paradox. He didn't think too much of women as musicians, and yet there were two women pianists I frequently heard Sun Ra praise, Dorothy Donegan and Mary Lou Williams." [A Strange Celestial Road, p 120]

And then there was the question what was the relationship of venues like these to the citadels of mainstream culture like, let's say,

Lincoln Center. Do they exist outside the cultural pipeline as [autonomous, confined, obscure, liberated] venues. Was this an autonomous space rich in creative ferment—subversive and independent. Were the musicians pitted against each other. Who would be selected, highlighted, their talent validated, celebrated by the cultural machine. And when and if the music reaches into the cultural mainstream is it absorbed and transformed in some negative way. Or in very positive ways reaches and impacts much larger numbers of people. Or some combination of all the above.

Throughout the book we see musicians change in very dramatic ways. As they transform themselves, laying claim to their space in a society structured to control and humiliate and diminish them. And inside the groups themselves the tensions between leaders of a band and the others in it, between those who have, will have a large public following and those who do not and will not, is explored with great love and sensitivity and pain and at times anger.

Ahmed grapples with these deep clashing [forces, contradictions]. He rests inside those spaces and others like it, with great humanity as well as with humility and self-reflection. If people can tolerate the deep discomfort of those spaces and don't immediately need a way to escape from them, I think far reaching forms of awareness, change and resistance are possible.

My friend Lana Povitz is writing a book about Shulamith Firestone who was one of my all time closest friends. Her project has brought Shulamith vividly back to me. Among the things she will write about will be the early days of radical feminism. My strong guess is, but I would not remotely presume how she will go about doing it, the structural oppression in the society and the fault lines inside the response to it will be looked at, explored and discussed. The burning hot intensity of Shulamith and the other women in the first rush of insight and awareness that ignited the second wave of the women's movement. The breathtaking connections made at dizzying speed, as awareness and understanding just kept multiplying almost by the second. Then the implosion and crackups that followed. Many of the same issues—personal/political/structural —that are explored in Ahmed's book, some in different guises along with some that are very different, will also I think be discussed.

As if in a call and response to Ahmed's description of Sun Ra's views on women, in her first draft of chapter one, Lana quotes Shulamith saying:

"Though men in general believe women in general to be inferior, every man has reserved a special place in his mind for the one woman he will elevate above the rest by virtue of association with himself. Until now the woman, out in the cold, begged for his approval, dying to clamber onto this clean well-lighted place. But once there, she realizes that she was elevated above other women not in recognition of her real value, but only because she matched nicely his store-bought pedestal. Probably he doesn't even know who she is (if indeed by this time she herself knows)."

*

I am writing this shortly after the Oct 7 massacre by Hamas in Israel and the mass slaughter and destruction in Gaza by Israel.

One of the very few places I can turn to where people are talking about it with any real seriousness is Democracy Now. People being interviewed clearly trust the consciousness and integrity of host Amy Goodman and co-hosts Nermeen Shaikh and Juan González.

In addition to what is being reported an extra layer of horror is watching someone interviewed one day —a reporter, an aid worker, a thirteen year old girl whose legs have been amputated —and learn a few days later that that that person often along with their entire family has been murdered by an Israeli bomb or soldier.

As the carnage mounts even some writers in the mainstream press are beginning to speak with rare seriousness and concern. In cases of reporters who have been killed it is hard to know whether they have been specifically targeted or their death is more a random part of the wholesale carnage taking place.

One thing I have noticed that in listening to Democracy Now there is very little interchange among those interviewed. The positions that people take seem at times subtly, at other times markedly, different from each other. The large outlines of what is said are similar: serious revulsion and opposition to the Israeli orgy of violence in Gaza, criticism (with various degrees of intensity) of the Hamas massacre and the taking of hostages, long standing opposition to the Israeli occupations of Gaza and the West Bank, condemnation of settler violence with the complicity of the Israeli military and government on the West Bank. Everyone agreeing and calling for an immediate ceasefire as a minimal demand they all can agree on. Now does the way people speak reflect real differences, differences that can lead to very different outcomes down the line?

Shulamith once told me that bitter skirmishes over seemingly small differences taking place on the outer margins can widen as they work their way from the margins to the [mainstream, center] of what people will focus on in the future. At which point those differences can magnify and widen, often impacting the shape, focus and direction of a movement. So are these differences just questions of semantics or differences that seriously portend very different, and if history is any guide, often tragic outcomes.

As important as what people say, is what they don't say. And it is always important to pay attention to both. Though often enough you might not be clued in until way later to what was left out.

Something not said could be an oversight, or someone might think it is implicit to what they are saying. It might only be different words used to express shared outrage and pain. Also someone might not want to say something that feels like they are capitulating to bad faith objections and being trapped or folded into an agenda they are actively resisting. It also can be a form of conscious misdirection or outright manipulation. Or can lead someone to think they know more than they do about what is happening. Also words and ideas don't remain static. As more people are exposed to them they can start to take on different meanings. And powerful ideas often get coopted, absorbed, transformed. The liberatory power of those words reduced, diluted. So as a result people often talk past each other.

I think there has to be a place where these differences can be discussed. Right now as things grow increasingly more dire everyone on the show seems to implicitly agree that in the midst of unspeakable horror that discussion will have to wait.

There is one thing about the show that has over the years seriously upset me. It is kind of what the new poetry calendar was trying to achieve writ large. Other than where it is important to know, like if someone is a doctor in a hospital that is being bombed, people are way too often introduced by the status conferred on them by powerful corporate institutions: award winning writer, long time Harvard Law professor, best selling novelist, Dean of the Media Department at MIT, star of the new hit Netflix series, winner of the prestigious Booker prize, Three time Emmy award winner, Nobel Prize recipient in biology, Pulitzer prize winning, Recipient of the prestigious MacArthur grant, Acclaimed World Renowned ... Golden Globe nominee for their role in." All said with a flourish that seriously reinforces the potency of those institutions in giving them the legitimacy to determine who will be listened to or not. Achievement means institutional and corporate validation of what you've done. And who should be paid attention to. All the more disturbing because the people themselves are serious, socially/politically engaged, often physically courageous and have important things to say. The intense stratification creates a kind of animated docility where your thoughts, opinions, curiosity, commitments are validated, yet simultaneously you are over and over again being told to know your place.

*

There was a documentary called Shulie made in 1967 that surfaced a couple of years ago. It was about the then 22 year old Shulamith Firestone in art school. She speaks of a life she wants to live where every word, every brush stroke is infused with meaning. It was about a year or two before all of everything started clicking into place for her. She doesn't yet have crucial categories at her disposal, some of which she herself as well as others will create in the years to come. She is piecing things together with words and concepts that are available.

I think we are at a similar point right now. We are going to have to figure something out. Circumstances [might, could, should, will] force us to. Or if not we might be frozen in place. Or worse just ride the momentum to unexpected and grim places that our increasingly unexamined and significantly inadequate assumptions might take us.

On Turning 80

Between twilight and daybreak
Lovers who were never lovers
Come to me and say,
"You were always so clueless
How can someone be that dense."

Saw my ancient face in the mirror of the cafe. First time since the pandemic I didn't wear a mask inside. The first time that I bought coffee there that they could see my face. Ghostly, faded, my thinning hair powdery white. How do I deal with this ever growing older, old, old me.

At 79, this is the first year I said kaddish on my father's yahrzeit, the anniversary of his death, when I was older than he was when he died. Looking at him from this side of the divide I feel his vulnerability/fear. How he was only a younger version of me. In fact everything he ever did in his life he was younger than I am now.

A dream by Myrna Nieves:

I wake up, and miss many things, including my friend Ana and her curious face.

Sueño

My friend Ana came to me (she passed away years ago). I tell her:

—Ana, let's visit the past.

A whole world of people we knew shows up in a slightly blurry way. They move around and seem to be inside a room or several rooms. Our world is separated from that world by a thin transparent membrane or wall, like the one made by a bubble of soap. We enter the "bubble," which does not burst, and join a familiar world of 30 or 40 years ago. I tell Ana: "this is how we can visit any time frame, any place."

We look at the people in the world we entered, including us at that time, and delight on how lively and joyful they are. It is not blurry anymore. They cannot see us. We can watch, but not interact with them." There is so much passion and light on their faces. They are all beautiful, in the prime of their lives. I watch them more than I watch me. I am aware that I am there at that time, 40 years younger, but for some reason I mainly focus on the people I knew. They are not concerned with their bodies; if they look good and are healthy or not. They just are. Bright, alive, fully existing in the now.

I don't know how long we can stay in this time. We are just visiting, but I am also aware that there is no pressure to return to our world.

*

Ros Pechesky 81 year old professor arrested at a major Jewish Voice for Peace demonstration in Grand Central Station calling for a ceasefire in Gaza. I hadn't heard her name for over 40 years. I was so happy that she was still on the planet. I don't even know if we ever spoke. But I remember her as someone front and center in the struggle for reproductive rights. And I had a very vivid memory of how she looked. The next day I saw a clip of her being arrested. Her voice sounded different. She looks the way politically engaged older women looked when I was younger. The same commanding presence, commitment and unswerving purpose.

*

Dec. 2, 2023.
I turn 80.

I see people who I think I know. They have grown ancient. After the initial confusion I try to place them or more try to confirm my initial "could that be, that must be, is it." I recognize them by my general impression of them. I look for familiar mannerism, how they scratch their head, tap their feet. Maybe by their shoes. Often by something I never realized I had observed before.

I attended the birthday party of a friend who turned 88 at the rehab center where he was recovering from a fall. The place slowly filled up with members of a music group he was part of. A group whose concerts I have attended for decades. I heard someone say something about "D minor."

I sat sunk deep into a sofa, making groaning sounds, a bit exaggerated, whenever I had to get up. For years now I thought a recording of the sounds many of my friends and I make when we get up would be a huge worldwide hit. I guess mostly for a niche audience. But a huge, huge one at that.

I keep reading about what 80 looks like, feels like, is capable of being. For me the experiences of my childhood are growing further and further removed from what other people's childhood memories are. Even then all of our childhoods from the time I was a child were quite different. But still the differences across generations are pronounced.

I have a friend who is 37. While much of our thinking is very similar we have very different associations about who and what brought us into consciousness. Sometimes our conversation go too quickly and those differences don't fully register. In the sense I have a second conversation, always rich and interesting in my head after we separate. "What in fact did she mean by that? I think I responded too quickly." Many people she read and was influenced by, I knew as actual people. Some of whom she now knows in their older forms. And many of the wide range of people she knows and has engaged with are people I have never heard of.

That has always been the case. Even now as people keep dying, people I never knew or at best barely heard about, as I read about them, major blanks get filled in. Things of great importance were happening in and around me and off to the side as I was stumbling, sleep walking my way through the decades.

The last few years I have grown more distant, more removed, more cut off. A fear, an emotional lethargy, a sense of resignation intensified during the pandemic.

Illnesses related to age also loom large. Dread is a constant companion. But what I also do find very disturbing is the attempt to continually socialize me or imprison me into very demeaning social categories. Negative or positive stereotypes about how I look, what my desires have to be, what I am capable of and on and on and on about things that have absolutely nothing to do with who I am. Though a lot to do with what I have to contend with: the structural and personal ageism and bigotry that I am continually faced with. And in that way has had an impact on who I am. Not to absorb the bigotry coming at me is an effort that does change you.

*

One thing I have noticed is friends and family of friends that have died, people I felt close to, maybe not in the same way as to the friend who died, slip away. I make some efforts to stay in touch. But those don't take hold. The pandemic I think played some role in this. Before, I might be invited to a gathering, a party, a seder as a way to stay in touch. But when those stopped, all contact basically stopped also. This hasn't always been the case. Things are a bit more fluid than that. But it has happened more than I expected. It has not been hurtful in the sense of feeling rejected (well maybe a little). But painful in the sense of missing them.

*

A quiet death, a painful death, a violent death, an accidental death, a drawn out death, a whatever death—expired is a word that seems to describe the state right after your last breath. Maybe that's too tame a word to describe a violent death. Your first breath at birth is the one you breathe in. Another thing I learned just recently.

*

A sudden scream of anguish and dread coming out of me in the middle of the night bolting me upright in my bed. A groggy, worried voice from the other room asking me if I were okay. I reassure her that I was.

Death terror seized me. With a rawness I haven't experienced since I was in my early teens. Not the *when* of my death or the *how* of my death. But the very fact of it. Periodically that terror seizes me again. The reality of it, the unreality of it. Not as fiercely as that night. But there nevertheless.

At some point as a teenager the death terror left me. I actually remembered the sense of relief I experienced when it was replaced by other fixations and pain.

Now sixty five years later it is back again.

Right after I wrote those last words, I wrote a comment to the Times, very tangentially related to an article I had barely glanced at, "Easter 2050. Here's What American Religion Looks Like" by Ross Douthat. I was surprised that they actually published my comment. Even more surprised when one of my favorite commenters (a reader who responds in the comment section to articles in the paper) responded to what I wrote. We kept going back and forth, the paper still publishing our exchange, even as we moved further and further away from the original article.

Even though a bit lighthearted, my own state of mind was very unsettled when my initial comment sprung out of me. I think it was a way to neutralize the actual unsettled state I was in. The intensity of my emotions were more visceral than my words would indicate. I often write about very intense emotions as well as very scary, unsettling situations. But this was different. The very act of writing and reading my fellow commenter's responses triggered panic. After one exchange I lay down and for about thirty seconds images kept fracturing, spinning and spinning ever faster in my head.

The Exchange:

Robert Roth
NYC 4h ago

60 years ago I was 20. In 60 years I will 140. Time moves fast and slow.
9 REPLIES

617to416
Ontario via Massachusetts 4h ago

@Robert Roth Or, if you look at it another way, you'll have reached infinity—or maybe negative infinity.

Robert Roth
NYC3h ago

@617to416 Since it might be my forever future what do you mean by negative infinity.?

Robert Roth
NYC2h ago

@617to416 Have been thinking and writing (at least trying to write) a lot about that recently.

617to416

Ontario via Massachusetts 2h ago

@Robert Roth I guess if you're religious, it's infinity—eternal existence. And if you're not religious then maybe it's eternal nonexistence?

617to416

Ontario via Massachusetts 1h ago

@Robert Roth On immortality (or the lack thereof)? I've always thought that the infinity of the universe focuses briefly into a point that is our individuality and then, when we die, that point dissolves back into the infinity of the universe. Or something like that ... I think this is why I've always been drawn to Wordsworth's poetry.

"....And I have felt

A presence that disturbs me with the joy

Of elevated thoughts; a sense sublime

Of something far more deeply interfused,

Whose dwelling is the light of setting suns,

And the round ocean and the living air,

And the blue sky, and in the mind of man:

A motion and a spirit, that impels

All thinking things, all objects of all thought,

And rolls through all things."

Robert Rothat 80
NYC50m ago

@617to416 Thanks. Sort of right where I left off this morning. Might quote you in my piece.

617to416
Ontario via Massachusetts 37m ago

@Robert Roth I'd be honoured—and would love to read it.

617to416
Ontario via Massachusetts 16m ago

@617to416 Oh, and I'd also say that philosophically there's something in my thinking very close to the idea from the Bhagavad Gita of the self (atman) yoked (yoga) to the self of all beings (brahman). So Wordsworth and Krishna ...

Robert Roth
NYC 3m ago

@617to416 definitely grateful the infinity of the universe focused briefly into a point where we could have this exchange.

Robert at 80 [Written when I was 65]

WHAT A PATHETIC LIFE I LEAD
A German filmmaker in her 70s
A Zimbabwean woman in her 20s
Love them both
Wildly attracted to each
Have no chance with either

"I'm a very good lover, a terrific friend and a lousy boyfriend." I would say this to women and it worked like a charm and more often than not we would have sex. An anarchist poet living in the Village. Sometimes that's what it would be. We would keep it that way. A bit impersonal, more impersonal maybe than it should have been. It created a space of excitement and had an allure of freedom. Sometimes my actual talent would disrupt the fantasy. "Hey, you write beautifully" with a slight surprise that was always a bit hurtful. But still I enjoyed it. It moved from a kind of cool "impersonality" in playing out a fantasy, to a subtle but real distancing which while at times disorientating was not the worst thing. Because I thought it was still mostly play acting and not all that impersonal. And I said what I said with conviction because I thought it was true. But unfortunately emotions crept in. Jealousy. Possessiveness, expectations etc. One lover said, "I have the worst of both situations. I'm too caught up with you to have other lovers. And I don't have the security that a commitment would give me." And that was it in a nutshell. Not exactly a nutshell. Because it doesn't include my own insecurities and jealousy. Once I understood that I really couldn't follow through I could not say it again. It would have just been a line, a lie to get sex. And without conviction it wouldn't have worked anyway. So I stopped saying it. Have not really been able to figure out what to say or do since.

My downstairs neighbor. A very thin dark brown woman always spectacularly dressed. A Mohawk haircut and an aura so bright it lights up the stairs or the street, always bringing a big smile to my face. Before we actually met I saw her talking to a tender, muscular man who works in the restaurant on the ground floor of my building. His father had recently died and he had been away for quite a while to be with his family. They stood in the vestibule, her empathetic face filled with emotion, her heart wide open and present. A couple of months later we spoke. A fashion designer from Zimbabwe with magic, soulfulness, tenderness and wild, brilliant perceptions. My head spins whenever we are together. What can I have with her, a woman in her 20s maybe early 30s, who wants to get married and have children. And who doesn't want anything interfering with the plan.

There is nothing I can say at 64. If I were 28 or 33 or 42 I wouldn't have wanted children any more than I do now. And I certainly never wanted to get married. A younger me now would probably be different than the younger me then. Who knows how and in what way. But for better or worse it is this older me that's at issue. What would I need to change in myself to have even a remote chance of being lovers with her?

Friends with benefits? My feelings for Aziza too intense and complicated for that. Fuck buddies? There is I guess a difference between fuck buddies and friends with benefits. Fuck buddies might in fact be easier. More straight forward. More direct. Why? I don't know why. Just felt like saying it. Though I haven't heard that term for a while. Francesca's fuck buddy moved into her apartment after 9/11. He came over the night before and it was two years before he left. What starts out as friends with benefits often winds up on Court TV. At 65 being Aziza's "boy toy" is probably out of the question. But then again stranger things have happened.

I think again of my beautiful downstairs neighbor. For the first time age really comes in on me. I think of myself at 80. That is just 15 years away. Though 50 was a while ago. And what does she need with that? And how then can this intimacy be expressed without committing her to the possibility of tending to an old man. Obviously anything can happen to anyone at any time. But here there is an almost certain future if I live that long. A commitment to each other would take that into account. Eighty though is still potentially very vibrant and very sexual. Another reason monogamy as an ideal is shit. With some real fluidity between us whatever sexual connection we had would not limit her to it. Me neither I guess. But in this case it would be her I would be most concerned about. Why am I obsessing and fretting about something that is very unlikely to happen? I guess because it's fun to do.

Months later. We speak about one weekend before we became good friends, when she was still living downstairs, when she cut herself off from everyone and everything. No email. No phone. A four day urban retreat, looking deep into herself, trying to find a "purpose," a direction, a deeper meaning, a deeper pursuit. I tell her about a small cottage on the top of a hill somewhere in Zimbabwe where I imagine living when I'm 80. In my fantasy Aziza has created some space for me on a large plot of land that is dedicated to some very significant pursuit. Maybe a place for children. Maybe something entirely different.

"What will you do there?" she asks. "Well, I'm there. That should be enough," I answer. "You have to do some work," she laughs."You can't just live there." "I'll be a presence. What more do I have to do?" "A presence *is* more than enough," she answers, yielding to the power of my argument. And so there it is. My future. A cottage on a hill in Zimbabwe. The destination a certainty. The route getting there very much a mystery.

Walking toward the East Side I come to Greenwich and 10th where there is a fork in the road. Totally forgot where I am going, who I am visiting. A total absolute blank. This has happened a few other times recently. Two times at that very spot. Scary feeling. Tried to relax. The destination returned and I continued. At 80. Hot muggy Zimbabwe summer. Wild committed energy everywhere. Up and down the hill. Not knowing where I am. Which direction I am going. Maybe this is something that will happen from time to time. Hopefully no more than that.

The total blank was very scary. Maybe try to surrender to it next time.

My father at 76 had sold his business, but still tried making deals, still overflowing with energy. "You're still wheeling and dealing," I said. "I'm doing more wheeling than dealing," he replied.

Postscript:

At 73 I might have a whole new future. There was a magnificent *Times* Op-Doc [documentary] focusing on a heavy set black woman in her thirties who had taken up pole dancing. She was beyond graceful. She was strong, limber, just shining with energy, focus, charm and determination. She spoke of the racist, sexist body shaming forces she had to overcome in pursuing her pole dancing career. In addition to performing she had started a pole dancing school.

Here's a link to the video. The comment section seems to have disappeared. So I reproduce the exchange we had below the link.

http://www.nytimes.com/2016/12/06/opinion/dangerous-curves.html?comments#permid=20725831[1]

NYC December 7, 2016

I just turned 73. Was wondering what I should do to strengthen my body and increase my flexibility. Admittedly from this chair to a pole might be a long trek. But then again...

Roz The Diva

Brooklyn December 8, 2016[2]

---

1. **http://www.nytimes.com/2016/12/06/opinion/dangerous-curves.html?comments#permid_43ec3e5dee6e706af7766fffea512721_2072583 1**

Robert, I'd be HONORED to have you in my class. HONORED. I'm not kidding at all. Hit up my website to see my schedule: rozthediva.com/schedule[3]

I was walking on air for two days.

A recently discovered fragment called Endless Footnotes *has been authenticated as being original Roth writings. Evidence is very strong it was written at a point in his life that his usual melancholy and fears and terrors were in a heightened state. We still do not know what* Endless Footnotes *was in reference to. But it does provide an important window into his life at a very vulnerable and critical point. Though not knowing what they are in reference to greatly limits what we can confidently deduce from them.*

What we are less sure of are the thousands of comments written under his name that appeared in the long defunct New York Times, *a popular news source of the period.*

Many of these comments have identifiable elements of Robert's own writing. But there is much speculation that most if not all of them were not written by him. That they were in fact generated by an early version of AI. The slight variations in the focus of the comments seem like primitive attempts at making them look genuine. But they feel very much like programmed variations, not anything real. They don't even have the flattened out monotone of some of his other writings. The arid sound of the words devoid of any real music would likely be due to early AI program inadequacies. The comments quoted in Endless Footnotes *do in fact seem genuine. Though it could be an attempt at humor, a wry form of counter appropriation, using what was meant as a form of undermining*

---

2. https://www.nytimes.com/2016/12/06/opinion/dangerous-curves.html#permid_43ec3e5dee6e706af7766fffea512721_20725831_853ae90f0351324bd73ea615e6487517_20735329

3. *http://rozthediva.com/schedule*

his integrity or was conversely an attempt to piggyback on his reputation, and by turning it on its head, claiming the words are his own. And by that very claim giving them a relevance that otherwise would not be there.

What is very clear, and this everyone agrees on, none of it could have been written by another Robert Roth. The cliches repeated and repeated over and over again—even if computer generated—were personalized cliches very particular to him.

*****

I'm having the hardest time with this next section. It goes on in so many directions at once. Maybe just saying it out loud will help. It is about different ways I have been written about, sometimes by name, sometimes as an inspiration for a fictional character, sometimes in poetry, sometimes in prose, as well as ways I have written about others and myself. Where it is all made up, where the emotional truth is pretty accurate but none of the facts are, where it all goes off the rails.

Some versions of me, not by name, appear, for example, in poems by Louise Rader. Once, while reading a new book by her, a collection of poems each in the form of a single sentence, the following poem brought me up short.

NOT JUST LUST SENTENCE [*Hmm*]

With female soft murmuring upstairs

the man's hourly Tourette cries have

mutated to whispers and I think how

could she on those crusty sheets by

a towering heap erupted cascade of

envelopes crucifixes on walls seen

when a locksmith toiled there but

what of my long ago lover on 13th near [O*h damn. That's me*]

Avenue B whose floor tumbled in cast

aside layers of typed brilliance our [*wait*]

anarchist hot-lava-lust sloshing toward

his newsprinted bed my compulsive

aesthetic cleanliness flung to the fire [*okay*]

escape rail until the uptown bus a not

quite Kafkaesque cockroach emerging [*EEEk! Damn! I didn't know that*!]

from my burgundy velvet bag to pause

beside leaves of the shocking pink [*Oh God! Come on!]*

embroidered rose as I stifled screams

to brush off attention determined never [*I guess I can see how that could be off-putting*]

to return to that squalor of gouged out

plaster yet drawn to it again and again

a huge post-modern painting unblessing [*What happened to that painting?*]*

forth though a sense of our golden touch. [*That part I remember*]

*A painting by Charlotte Hastings. It was an explosion of brilliant color and energy. My aunt Claire compared it to an orgasm. Sadly, very sadly the painting got irreparably damaged decades ago.

Louise Rader whose storied career as a poet, tax resister, psychotherapist, dancer is well chronicled in the recently discovered Breath and Brilliance *an anthology of poet activists in the upper Northeast of what was then the United States, now an alliance of interconnected self-sustaining communities. Published in the late 21st century, it provides a comprehensive sweep of the creative forms of resistance from the early 1900s to the time the book came out. The chief archivist from Transitional Upheaval an organization chronicling historical epochs in the midst of major transformations called me with the discovery. Keeping with the traditions of the period Rader referred to her artist endeavors as a spiritual calling. A close textual reading of her huge oeuvre has identified a handful of poems that very likely were about her romantic relationship with Robert. There is a subtle at times marked shift in the breath and cadence of the poems when writing about him.*

*

Diana Liben gave me a piece of paper with a key to the real world identities of thinly veiled characters in Delmore Schwartz's *The World Is a Wedding*. Many of whom, including Meyer Liben her former husband still friend who died a few years before, had become very prominent literary/political figures in the 50s, 60s. People whose work and reputations have faded over the years. Though the influence of their work is still with us today. Occasionally someone writes a book or makes a documentary and that period comes alive again, at least for a short time. One character in *The World is a Wedding* is The Kid. I would see the person it was based on at the annual Christmas party thrown by the daughter of another person appearing as a major fictional character in the story. Over the years I would see The Kid occasionally walking around the Village. Well into and past middle age, he had a bounce and buoyancy to his walk that always conjured up the image of The Kid to me. We would say hello and chat for a minute or two. "The World isn't a Wedding" he laughed retelling the story the one time I brought it up.

I have no idea where that list is. The information on that list is in fact historically valuable. It could still be buried in some drawer along with Herschel Walker's signature on an attendance sheet he signed as a student in my friend's philosophy class at Georgia University. At the time he was the most famous college football player in the country. My friend, who herself has become an influential social political thinker (fictionalized aspects of her have flitted in and out of my own work over the years) gave attendance sheets after the semester with Hershel's signature/autograph on them as gifts to her friends. She said Herschel would hold court in class, the young white women in particular hanging on his every word. And if he had a notion, it would remain fixed in his brain (my friend called it idée fixe) and nothing said could shake him from it. A trait that has grown infinitely more extreme and disastrous over the years. I visited my friend in Georgia at the time and we sat on the grass outside the packed stadium. We stayed for a while as we listened to the public address announcer describe what happened after each play: Herschel Walker seven yard gain over left tackle. First down.

Lana Povitz is writing a biography of Shulamith Firestone. In the course of doing her research Lana came across an unpublished novel that Shulamith wrote. *The Adventures of Faygi and Jude in Amerika.*

Desire. Disappointment. Massive tragedy. Massive horror. It covers decades of life, struggle, awareness, pain. It is the story of two women deeply, often bitterly locked into each other's lives. Lana, Shulamith's sister Laya Seghi (so similar to her sister in poignant, profound ways) and I spent some time discussing the book.

One interesting aspect of our conversation was moving back and forth to the sources of some of the events written about and keeping in mind that these were characters in a novel and not the literal story of Shulamith's life. Lana and Laya agreed that both women Faygi and Jude each represented different dimensions of the massive reality of who Shulamith was.

I suspect for Lana, who is writing Shulamith's biography, the novel offers a treasure trove of clues. And my own admittedly prissy and unprovoked bringing up a couple of times that we should remember this is fiction no matter how closely resembling real events it might be, was more trying to protect my own blurring of lines in the fiction I've written than anything Laya and Lana were saying. In addition hearing Laya's response to fictionalized events that were based on real fraught interactions between Laya and Shulamith that had dire real world consequences was straight out riveting. As is her soulful, deeply searching, at times harrowing, eulogy written about her sister.

In my case, the fiction I wrote when I was in my 30s was about people straddling an alternative, insurgent radical world and a mainstream world they were significantly, militantly in opposition to. Yet in some serious, often unexamined ways, were still a captive of. Living lives both of resistance and compliance.

In my long short story *In the Audience*, a short story with the feel of a novella, many of the characters were composites of people I knew. Some are just totally made up. Those that resemble or were seriously based on real people were not remotely written about in the same way as if I were writing about the actual people themselves. They do take on independent lives. I did try and change their physical appearance.

And I did make up situations that they found themselves in. Now what was interesting is that people who didn't know who inspired my characters often recognized people in their own lives who were similar to them. And the characters I created or who created themselves felt very distinct and alive to me. In another book *Health Proxy* written much later which some called a novel, some called a memoir, I saw it more as an extended meditation. I mixed fiction with real events. There were times I used someone's real name, other times when writing about the same person I might use a made up name or no name at all, presenting them as an entirely different person.

Maxwell Berman, one of the major characters in *In the Audience* was in many ways an exaggerated version of myself. Unlike me though, Maxwell says the first two things that come to mind rather than have a third thought that undercuts the other two. So the energy of original insight just flies out there. Allison one of the other characters was in a large part inspired by my friend Muriel Dimen scholar, theorist, therapist, poet, song writer, political activist whose transcendent brilliance infused so much of her work and so much of her life. In the story there is an intense push pull between Allison and Maxwell that parallels the early days of our relationship.

"During the first months of their friendship Maxwell and Allison would meet every couple of weeks for half an hour or forty-five minutes, usually in the late afternoon in a coffee house or restaurant. They would meet in a space in Allison's tight, carefully structured schedule. Maxwell who had less to do could more or less be the one to accommodate.

"Their meetings were often tense and peculiar. They would speak past each other. They would both be dull. Allison would look up at the ceiling. Maxwell would talk past her shoulder. Allison would withdraw. Maxwell would grow panicky and start speaking compulsively, speaking loudly with uncharacteristic bravado. And the more Maxwell would talk the more Allison would withdraw. And the more she would withdraw the more he would talk. Allison would feel she was drowning or she was being consumed. Once, in the street, she grabbed her chest and grew faint. "Please, no more," she demanded. Whenever he left her Maxwell would feel relieved. It's not worth it, he would think. And then a half hour later he would be flooded with affection and longing....

One day Maxwell blew up. "I'm always in the interstices of your life," he said with a flourish. "I'm neither your friend nor your colleague. I'm neither in your public life nor your private life."

Allison answered, "There are certain things, very intimate things, that I can tell you. Other things I make a conscious decision not to. It must be painful and confusing. Our conversations are stilted. There is something twisted in our friendship." And with a flourish of her own, "From now on I will be consistently less intimate." [*In the Audience*]

Soon after I wrote the story I gave a reading, The reading lasted about 45 minutes. Arnie said all through it he watched Muriel who previously had read the story, pacing up and down the aisle of the auditorium, shaking her head, nodding her head, laughing, looking annoyed, knitting her brow, laughing, smiling, grimacing, shaking her head, nodding, laughing.

Another time, much later, in what may have been the best reading I ever gave, Muriel was sitting next to Stephanie Hart. They didn't know each other. In this case the pieces I read had nothing at all to do with Muriel. Stephanie said Muriel was totally involved in my performance. Slow down, stand up straighter, what a good line, I never read that one before. Project your voice, why did you have to read that one! Stephanie said she couldn't stop laughing to herself. Like Arnie, she got totally lost in Muriel's reactions and couldn't exactly listen to my reading. And like way too many things, as much as I knew it, I didn't really appreciate or understand or ever fully take in how deep Muriel's love for me was.

*

A fictional character named Robert Roth appears in the novel *The Cutting Edge* by David Lansky.

The novel is divided into two parts. The first is The College Essays of Jenny Delight. No one is quite sure who Jenny is. It is an obvious pseudonym since there is no student by this name at the college, a community college on Long Island. It is a hilarious section laced with social and personal insight as Jenny tries to understand the world around her, often using categories she's learning, sometimes the most abstract categories available, and infusing them with vivid meaning. The second section, Bill of Sale, is the posthumously-discovered manuscript of Sociology Professor Fred Snyder. It is a harrowing account of very vulnerable and often screwed-up people who are totally against their society. It is a section revealing, with extraordinary power, the ruthlessness of contemporary capitalism and its relentless destructive force.

Robert Roth is an anarchist poet and editor of a small literary magazine called *And Then*. Even though he appears only on rare occasions, he cuts an impressive figure. Other than a slightly below the surface resemblance to me, there are noticeable differences between us. Which in no way diminished the thrill I felt whenever he popped into the story.

As for David Lansky the author, that really is the pseudonym used by the radical sociologist and poet George Snedeker who at the time was teaching sociology at a community college on Long island.

How am I expected to figure any of that out? Who's real, who's not real. What's fiction, what's a memoir, what's a scrap of paper with scribblings on it.

In the case of Robert, not the fictional Robert but the actual Robert, by his own admission he was not a reliable narrator, a popular term among academics and literary critics of the time. He learned the term late in life and said as categories go it describes him perfectly.

No way to say it other than just say it outright. People were totally confused back then. Confusion was an emotion I learned about in Advanced Research Studies, but never experienced until now. Everyday I sound more and more like Maxwell Berman. How do you experience Stockholm syndrome with a fictional character and not a malevolent one at that. I feel like I am a total captive of his anxieties, of his consciousness. Fortunately everyone has reassured me that this is only a temporary condition.

And then there is Robert Roth, stealth deus ex machina, appearing here and there in a memoir being written as we speak. This Robert is also a fictional character. I met the writer L.K. Madrid a decade after the period written about. In the book Robert swoops in when there is an insoluble problem that needs attending to. For example when L.K. is writing about times he was out of the country and wanted to include things that were happening elsewhere, fictional Robert is brought in to give a first person account of having been there. Or if not there, he might repeat what others have told him or how the underground press had covered it. Or if the political tensions of the era needed to be explored, described or shed light on, Madrid engaged in mock discussions with me where I had to get into character and become the fictional Robert Roth. Sometimes he would say things I might actually have said at the time, other things that I would never have said but L.K. wanted that perspective articulated in the book. That was something he was always very particular about. Some of those discussions, some of the very best ones, have already been cut from the book because the book was getting too long and unwieldy.

I*n Madrid's groundbreaking masterpiece we see early examples of Roth's thinking. Scattered through the book are crucial discussions between the two of them. While some of Roth's thoughts are all over the place and at times appear to contradict each other we see the genesis of ideas that will take form later in life. Ideas that have passed down through the generations and are, in only slightly altered forms, still with us today.*

***

These jottings were found on scraps of paper buried under water damaged notebooks in an abandoned warehouse in Red Hook, a breakaway region in the former United States.

A visitor came to see my mother in the hospital. Someone whom she has spoken to for years on the phone. A woman younger than myself, the daughter of a friend of my mother's who had a four year ending badly painful affair with a psychoanalyst, a "brilliant charismatic" man who touched her in deep and profound places. Places, she said that her husband could never reach. At the time she told her husband straight out about what was happening; he still wanted to be with her but she told him that she had to leave him. After her breakup with the psychoanalyst she returned to her husband. From time to time, she still sees the ex-lover who has grown very old and frail and helps take care of him.

My mother suddenly very alert waded headlong into the conversation, constantly referring to the ex-lover as "That son of a bitch." In truth her words seemed to grow more out of loyalty than real conviction. But when Ruth insisted that she wasn't a passive victim in the affair, that it was something that she chose to do, my mother answered that charisma was a powerful allure and people with it have some responsibility for its power. Back and forth. Great discussion about love, life, and desire.

*

I remember a conversation with Kirk Sale who wrote a book about SDS. I was friendly with him. I was close to his wife Faith Sale who along with Joyce Johnson had organized a writers group at the Free Association. Two other people Steve Fried and Ann Rower also conducted a writers group there. Both in different ways helped me start writing again.

One time Kirk invited me to a talk he was going to give. For some reason I couldn't make it. I think, though I may have come up with other ways to justify it to myself, but as I vaguely remember it, it was a decision not to go. A decision in the sense I could have dragged myself there but I was either too exhausted or depressed to go. Not that I had to be somewhere else. I didn't think he would care. He was genuinely upset I hadn't come. Not knowing your own power or importance to another person can lead to hurting them in ways totally unintended.

Though as I write this, one real shameful act on my part is flooding back to me. Knowing, but maybe not fully knowing, but how could I not know, I talked myself into thinking that it would be okay to do something else than go to a party I had agreed to go to. I convinced myself of all the reasons it wouldn't matter. I didn't know the man that well, I did have something that really mattered to me to go to which I found out about after I agreed to go to his party, there was no way to do both, or it would have been too difficult to do both, he wouldn't really care, so on and so forth. I was very apologetic when I called to cancel. It was creepy self-serving bullshit on my part. I knew it was important to him that I be there. The person was deeply, seriously wounded by it. It was like I had punched him in the stomach. And there really was no way to undo it.

*

One similarity between Arnie and Shulamith was both could, in Shulamith's case particularly when she was younger, put all their focus, very intense all absorbing focus on a person they were talking to. If someone else was there they could be totally beyond ignored. Kind of obliterated as if they didn't exist. Never pleasant under normal circumstances. Both because of the power of their personality and/or the power of their fixation it could be incredibly hurtful. I think it was a kind of extreme obliviousness on their part. Not everyone felt negated of course. But it could create real seething anger and sometimes long-lasting bitterness.

*

When Arnie and I did our first reading together, Bayard Rustin and Igal Rodenko both came and asked if people could comment afterwards. I was so tense and nervous and also worried that we would be upstaged by these extraordinarily gifted charismatic beyond brilliant speakers, that once they spoke all the attention would move in their direction. Arnie was more than okay with it. He was far saner than I was about it. But in his case he was more preoccupied whether someone he was totally in love with would show up or not. All through his part of the reading any sound coming from the back of the room would cause him to pause and look at the door to see if they had come. As for my saying no to Bayard and Igal, I won't say it was exactly stupid because I was so insecure. But it was an example where insecurity can radically undermine something that would benefit you in a big way. If Bayard Rustin and Igal Roodenko spoke, as well as anyone else there who felt they wanted to speak, it would have added a dimension to the night that would have been outright spectacular. As they were leaving Bayard said, "Quite an experience."

*

I was standing with a group of other demonstrators outside the 1964 Republican convention in San Francisco. James Forman Sr. (I am almost certain it was him) very calmly laid out the various things we could do. He spoke of the dangers involved and the legalities of each. In no way did he try to subtly coerce us to do anything that we felt uncomfortable doing. Or take risks we didn't want to take. He was extremely respectful of everyone there. There was room to make whatever decision each of us needed to make.

As for me I infiltrated the Mississippi Scranton for President delegation. Someone else infiltrated the Alabama delegation. At some point we unfurled a banner that in dripping red letters said JUSTICE. A woman called out. "You're not from Mississippi." A man then firmly but not in any way violently, escorted me out of the convention hall.

My mother later told me she had seen me on television and thought, "Now what has he got himself into."

*

My father died on the day that Geraldine A. Ferraro was nominated to be the Vice Presidential candidate during the 1984 Democratic convention. He had lived his whole life and never saw a woman nominated to be a vice presidential candidate. It was something he would have been very excited about. Her husband, John Zaccaro, had once been my landlord. I paid $23 a month rent and the building was well kept. So all through all the negative things written about him over the years I always retained some residual affection. That is until way later John and Geraldine viciously forced a friend of a friend out of a brownstone they owned in Greenwich Village where he had lived for decades because they wanted it for their own use. He was very old and sick at the time. And died shortly thereafter.

*

There was an article in *The Sunday Times Magazine* stating that Denzel Washington was the sexiest black male entertainer or something like that. The writer made a point to say that Harry Belafonte did not have anything close to the same sizzling sex appeal. A couple of days later my friend gave me a ticket to attend *Richard the Third* in Central Park starring Denzel Washington. And right in the box next to me was a buoyant Belafonte with a friend all excited about Denzel and the play. "How could he not be hiding under the covers?" I laughed when I saw him. He had recently organized Nelson Mandela's visit to New York. I eavesdropped on their conversation. He knew so much about Shakespeare. All through the play I was trying to get up the nerve to ask him if he would write a short piece about Shakespeare for a small magazine my friends and I (still) put out. I never did get up the nerve to ask.

*

Listening closely to people with empathy and curiosity was one of Roth's most commented on attributes. Though along with genuine interest in the person, he was also looking for material for And Then. *So a passing comment in the midst of any discussion might catch his attention, and he would wait until there was an opening in the conversation to bring it up. Not knowing when something said might issue into a request started playing a role in any and every interaction with him.*

My friend Bennett Lerner, the great pianist, would drink a big bottle of Gatorade before a concert. It gave him a lot of energy. I would often tell people about this. Many years later, I spoke to him about it. He said he didn't remember doing it.

Five Stories That Have Never Made Their Way into the Pages of *And Then*

1. Emmet Durant grew up in Lake City, a small town in South Carolina. His father had been in the military. Originally, I had met him in New York where he worked as a bartender at the Annex located on the Lower East Side. He was white and the clientele at the bar was largely, though far from exclusively, Black.

Lake City was a small Southern town that had a segregated movie theater. There is a hole in how I remember the story. It went something like this, I think. Segregation was outlawed. But at the local movie theater, if a white person wanted to buy a ticket they could, while a

Black person would be told that the theater was sold out. Emmet was part of a group trying to integrate the theater. The strategy was to mill around with the crowd outside the theater and at a signal, two people, one Black, one white, would step forward and go to the ticket booth and attempt to purchase a ticket.

While Emmett was waiting his turn, an old white man who knew him since childhood, who had real affection for him, who always treated him kindly, started up a conversation about outside agitators stirring up trouble. Emmett listened politely, said a few words, and then it was his turn to step forward. As he moved to the ticket booth, he glanced back and saw the old man looking bewildered, hurt and betrayed.

I tried looking Emmet up on the Internet. His name wasn't there. I called up a Durant in the town that he once lived in. There were a number of Durants living in the area. I got an answering machine and didn't want to leave a message. If something had happened to him, I didn't want to have to have them tell me. I liked him so much and it was so long since we had contact.

2. The second piece involves Robin Walsh. I first saw Robin riding a motorcycle through the streets of Cambridge, MA. As a freshman at Radcliff, she was a long jumper with world class ability. At her very first meet, an unsanctioned event, she leaped beyond the sandpit and broke her ankle. Though she recovered, she could never compete at that level again. The sandpit was where it was because meet officials never imagined that a woman could jump that far.

3. The third story involves Richard Brown, whom I had known for years and with whom I had a warm acquaintanceship. We never really spoke, but we both always lit up when we saw each other. I remember him mostly from Broadway Charlie's, a bar I would hang out in. It was a bar that Gary Francis Powers would come to. Powers had flown the U-2 spy plane that was shot down by the Soviet Union in 1960. Here he would sit on a bar stool drinking silently for hours. Don't have any

other memories of him. Just an occasional figure out of the corner of my eye. And I also remember a broad-shouldered guy, rumored to be a hit man, who would sit at another part of the bar. He was a bit more gregarious. I saw him once lose his temper, but it didn't seem like it would escalate beyond that.

Richard was always quiet, not in a sullen or angry way. Didn't seem like he drank all that much. I didn't drink at all, just hung out with friends, some of whom did drink a lot. Richard had a sweetness and warmth about him. One afternoon, while I was sitting alone at a table, he asked if he could join me. It was the first time we were ever this alone with each other. He told me about having once been convicted of murder in a very public trial, months of New York Post headlines. He was sent to prison. Two detectives who were sure he was innocent spent the next two years gathering evidence that would eventually clear him.

Try looking up Robin Walsh and Richard Brown. Particularly Richard. I think he moved to California. I don't think it is even possible to count the number of Richard Browns who live in the country. The Robin Walshes, while not even remotely a close second, are way too numerous to track down. Maybe I could find Robin with some effort. Recently I got the address of a mutual friend from long ago. But I am far from sure.

Robin was a good friend. I spent one summer in Cambridge, MA. immersed in a world made up mostly of lesbians and gay men. One time, I spoke to Robin and told her that no one ever called me just to say hello. She called the very next day. I am still touched by the memory of that call. She was a singer as well as an athlete. She was straight out gorgeous with a playful sparkle in her eyes. She also played basketball, had a killer jump shot, and was an excellent swimmer for her college team. But it was as a long jumper that she excelled at a world-class level, and that would never be the same again.

4. The fourth story involves my friend Sharon. Once when we were teenagers, she told me, at an event at the local synagogue, that

she and two friends of hers, two young black men, the same age as her, got stoned smoking grass while hanging out in a Jewish cemetery and started scrawling graffiti on tombstones. She thought at the time that it was an ironic hoot that three kids who were as politically and emotionally aware as they were, three people you would least expect it from, would do such a thing. I always remembered that story. In part because it was very clear that what they did wasn't motivated by hate or malice but by stupidity and lack of awareness of the impact it might have. I thought that distinction was important to keep in mind. Once while visiting Jackson Heights for the High Holy Days, I ran into her walking with her mother. I pulled her aside and asked if she would be up to writing about it for *And Then*. Not exactly the smartest or most sensitive thing to do after not seeing someone for decades. But it was something I always was hoping she might write and reflect back upon. So it was still very alive and active in my mind. She said it never happened. And that was that.

5. The fifth story would have been a scoop of international importance, even if only a thousand or so people would have first seen it.

Someone I knew had possibly the most grotesque job of anyone I have ever met. He had been a medical technician in China. His job was to examine death row prisoners to see who had compatible organs for someone with influence and power who needed a transplant. He would then select that person to be executed. After the execution, he and his medical team would run out to immediately extract the organs for transplant. The story he was going to write was about selecting a seventeen-year-old prisoner who had been in prison since he was thirteen for murdering someone. In China, no one could be executed till they were eighteen. But because his organs were especially needed, they moved up the execution date. The piece was about to be completed when a front-page article in the *Times* spoke of rumors about the harvesting and trafficking of organs from executed prisoners in China. The writer panicked and thought there could be terrible consequences for his family in China if his piece was ever published.

Memories

https://www.youtube.com/watch?v=Gv0jrL3Uzpo

Shortly after Arnie's mother died he was in such a state of devastation I felt I needed to do something to try and help pull him out of it. I suggested we write a piece together called "Leslie Klein's Petition" where Leslie Klein would speak in front of a room of left intellectuals and activists, people Leslie felt insecure around, was always trying to impress, and demand to be paid attention to and be respected. I said Arnie, present the rawest version of yourself. What you would ask for if you weren't embarrassed to be totally vulnerable. The important thing to remember is that Leslie Klein should not necessarily be an unappreciated neglected genius but someone who like anyone else deserves to be celebrated, paid attention to and respected. The demands should be very modest but virtually unrealizable.

The name Leslie was chosen so you couldn't be sure if Leslie was a man or a woman. I had no idea how important that would be in how people responded. Some people read him as being a man. Others read her being a woman. One person read it simultaneously as two separate stories. I also later learned from my mother that Klein meant small. A couple of friends had just assumed that was why we had chosen the name.

As Arnie dictated the petition and the demands, I had to stop him a couple of times and told him to be less eloquent (something that was so much a part of him that it was almost impossible for him not to be). As I was writing it down I changed a word here and there in an effort to bring it more in line with what I had in mind. We looked at it and then made some small changes. Pete Wilson copy edited it, making the speech and demands more raw and basic.

To indicate that it was fiction we dated it sometime in the future. Something we had to keep doing since the future kept coming and going.

Arnie and I wrote this story in 1980.

Leslie Klein's Petition

The following speech was delivered at the Caucus for Radical Concern during a three day conference in Shimmel Auditorium, N.Y.U., in February 1985.

Several years ago the gay and feminist movements came along and introduced a new form of consciousness. Pain and anger were expressed over concerns that weren't thought about before. Feminists and gay activists spoke out with deep seriousness; they were ignored and belittled, but they insisted on the truth of their complaints and the validity of their demands. It was embarrassing and uncomfortable. It was a long process but much of what they said and did has been incorporated as a regular part of our thinking.

Now in that tradition I bring a new problem and a new concern, difficult and embarrassing once again, something that will cause confusion and hostility. Let me explain the background here much in the style of the earlier consciousness raising.

I live with my father in a middle class neighborhood. I go to the neighborhood park and people say to me: What do you do? How do you earn a living? I say I have significant contacts, people in an active intellectual ambiance, people whose work appears in the *Village Voice*, the *Nation*, the *New York Times Book Review* as well as several small periodicals devoted to social change. They say that sounds exciting. Does it pay? Are you respected? Do you enjoy being with those people? I say it is intense and exciting. I may be on the verge of something very big. But it's complicated; these things are hard to spell out exactly. As I say this to them I am filled with confusion and there is pain in my heart. I am telling only a half truth. I do have some connections. I know some people respect me, but I have no real sense of security and dignity.

I sit alone at home often frustrated and sad. I feel left out of everything: parties, study groups, conversations, meetings. Everything. Most of you never even phone me. I feel neglected. It is with this in mind that I come before you today. I feel extremely angry and frightened. I am also very embarrassed. What I am asking might seem presumptuous, but all such things will appear presumptuous at first. I repeat again that a legitimate response to what I ask might demand a new consciousness and outlook.

I can't seem to do coherent and sustained work. I try. Occasionally I do call up the talk shows on the radio and make an intelligent statement, and every so often I will write a reflective essay. I feel the neighbors mock me behind my back, and I use my contact with you to justify myself with them. But I really don't know how I am seen in your eyes. This is a problem, I think, for many among us, which makes it a problem for all of us. This is why I have chosen to present a formal petition. In doing so I feel hesitation and ambivalence. I don't know if I will be listened to. If I will be paid attention to or will be rejected and ignored. Also even if I am listened to I don't know how much trust I can feel.

If I am rejected and ignored I will be filled with pain, confusion and finally bitter rage. I will then likely reach out to all those similarly betrayed who will join me in my rage. I hope we will never have to come to this point.

Now I will offer an explicit set of demands that are particular to my situation, but hold out the possibility for a solution to the problems of isolation, neglect and abandonment that I have raised. It's not a rigid formula or blueprint. On the other hand, I would not want to whittle down the force and essence of the demands I am here proposing. I want the substance and essence of them preserved without dilution or compromise.

I would like a phone call once a month from a prominent person.

I would like to appear three times a year on significant panels.

I would like at least a couple of my reflective essays to be published in respected journals.

I would like a small weekend symposium devoted to a critical review of my work and its overall coherent pattern

However little or much writing I do must absolutely not be a criteria for attention or acceptance by members of the Caucus of Radical Concern.

Some people identified strongly with Leslie Klein. Others were annoyed. A couple of people were furious. It got published in three different places. Cultural Correspondence published it along with a striking graphic which some friends put up in their offices, others on their refrigerators.

One friend, a galvanizing, charismatic, deeply engaged radical feminist called me and said we should get together and talk about the piece. Over lunch she just tore into Leslie Klein. That she wanted to piggyback on the work of others. Undermine their achievements. That Leslie Klein was always (yes, she said always) whining and pleading while others were doing the heavy lifting. I was startled by the intensity of her remarks. At some point I mentioned that Marty Duberman playwright, social critic, gay rights activist, and world renowned historian told me he strongly identifies with Leslie Klein. My friend with a slightly perplexed, slightly grudging smile replied, "But he's the person you want to have call you once a month."

The piece itself took on a life of its own. Arnie and I had to surrender "ownership" of Leslie Klein. We had become, if anything, distant stodgy forbearers of Leslie Klein with just the most tenuous of connections. That is if anyone even remembered that we had written it.

"If I can't dance, I don't want to be part of your revolution." Jane Schroeder took Emma Goldman's declaration totally to heart, dancing and singing at demonstrations, parties, lectures, at almost any kind of gathering. At some point she took total possession of Leslie Klein. Most notably at one Socialist Scholars Conference where she handed out hundreds of copies of the petition that she had typed up and photocopied. She had slightly but not inconsequentially altered the text as well as the demands. While handing them out she introduced herself as Leslie Klein. The organizers of the conference had no idea how to respond.

This was way more than anything Arnie and I had imagined. One part of me was totally embarrassed watching her in action. Another part was outright awe struck and exhilarated by what she was doing with it.

A week after the conference I attended a panel discussion. Lucy Lippard, the great radical art critic, started to speak. As she began relating a story it slowly dawned on me that she was talking about Leslie Klein. She smiled at me. She spoke of seeing a woman whose name she didn't know handing out sheets of paper at the Socialist Scholars Conference. She said it might seem pathetic, or difficult to hear, but the woman was demanding that people pay attention to her, that she felt humiliated and unappreciated by the lack of recognition. Lucy said it is part of our work to create a society and a movement that deals with loneliness, despair, and the humiliation and injury of constantly being judged and evaluated.

As Lucy spoke I thought that maybe this was getting a little out of hand. It was disorientating to listen to. I started imagining, more than imagining, I was actually visualizing people in Tokyo and Warsaw and Sydney, Australia talking about Leslie Klein in whatever altered form, with whatever embellishments and alterations she/he/they had been transformed into. For a fleeting moment I was tempted to set the record straight. But that did seem ridiculous. More importantly I felt an overwhelming need to rush home and call Arnie and tell him all about it.

As I write this all these years later it occurs to me that Lucy maybe, just maybe knew what Jane had been doing, was, even now one week later, just playing along and extending the performance one step further. More likely, why more likely?, she was actually responding to Leslie Klein as a real person. Either way, Lucy underlined the importance of the issues raised.

In the early 1980s Lucy Klein, a woman wearing wild colorful outfits and various styles of broad brimmed hats appeared on the scene. No one knew where she came from, what her nationality was, her age or if she had any specific political affiliations. Rumors were that Lucy was from El Salvador or Guatemala. Others said she was here from Sydney, Australia. It was as if she appeared out of nowhere. She had a reputation of boldly questioning both "legitimate" and "illegitimate authority," a popular distinction often asserted at the time. She was known to be either relentless and irritating, or relentless and inspiring. No one knows whatever happened to her. She disappeared as suddenly as she had appeared. Her manifesto stirred deep emotions. Controversy followed her everywhere. But none of us have been able to locate even one copy of the original petition. Still even today whole books have been written about its impact. Different versions of the petition, each one claiming to be the original, had been passed down through the generations by word of mouth. Her manifesto has been alternately described as emblematic of a politics of scatter shot grievances or as one of liberation and transcendence. While still somewhat disputed, to me the evidence is overwhelming, that this was when the now ubiquitous expression "kleining it" *became part of everyday speech.*

Doctor's Report

Comments

80 year old male with PMH of hyperlipidemia, prediabetes, GERD, gout, and BPH presenting for a CPE.

> Hyperlipidemia: Tolerating statin therapy. Last LDL-C was 106 on atorvastatin 20 mg daily.

> Prediabetes: Last Hba1c was 5.9. Will monitor. Continue ADA diet.

> GERD: Controlled on PPI, omeprazole dosage has been reduced to 20 mg. Rarely symptomatic.

> Gout: Originally presented to the Northwell Emergency Department for left hallux swelling and redness. Was diagnosed with gout and prescribed indomethacin with improvement. Initial uric acid level was 7.2 and peaked at 8.3. Evaluated by rheumatology and was prescribed allopurinol and colchicine. On allopurinol 200 mg daily and is now off colchicine. No recent flares.

> BPH: Sees GU regularly and remains asymptomatic.

> HM: Due for a 2023-2024 COVID-19 vaccine. Eligible for RSV vaccination. Otherwise up to date. Lives alone and is able to attend to all ADLs.

> Rash over his left lateral ankle.

> Thinks he might have a splinter in his left foot.

Otherwise well.

Last edited by John Chuey, MD on 5/9/2024 9:48 AM.

Even then doctors had a way with words. An ability to catch one important part of the essence of what makes a person a person. The challenges they face, the accommodations they need to make, a window into how they are seen. An 80 year old Robert? How did he cope with all these things that were more than just words. Did he understand what any of it meant.

A possible splinter in his foot? Nothing better captures his poignant vulnerability and his tendency to fret and worry. As well as his ability to pull people into his world of concerns.

Enough already. I have had to suspend my exploration of the past. The impact of such deep immersion has disorientated me to a degree I hadn't expected. Just when you think you understand something you come across another piece of the puzzle and you have no idea where that will fit. Or even if it is the same puzzle. A doctor's report? Okay Okay. Does everything have to have a deep meaning or have crucial information or be infused with whatever it is supposed to be infused with.

Robert retreated from view for long stretches of time. Was he ill, was it depression, was it lack of access. Is that really true? Why do people keep asking me if it's true?

I myself have not been well. No one can identify the problem. I can't even describe what I am going through. Living through the past certainly doesn't guarantee me surviving the present.

*

The Personal and The Historical

A spectacular, stunningly beautiful designer from Zimbabwe stayed with me for about nine months. Priced out of the apartment below, our apartments were connected by a fire escape—our own urban duplex. She had nowhere else to stay. Her parents, first her father then her mother were ambassadors to another country. Overhearing her phone conversations mostly with her mother, occasionally with her father I heard her referring to Robert Mugabe in hushed deferential tones as The President. My cousin was friends with Henry Kissinger. So almost forever he had been this kindly uncle/mass murderer lurking somewhere in the shadows of my life. With Mugabe being here on a regular basis, Kissinger's presence became more pronounced. It was spooky having my small apartment filled with all this ghoulish world scale criminal energy.

*

In his small nondescript six floor walk up apartment in a neighborhood once teaming with artistic and insurgent political energy back channel negotiations between world leaders would surreptitiously take place. There was some curiosity among the neighbors who these late night visitors were. And an occasional sleepy annoyance yelled into the intercom when someone—often a head of state—pushed the wrong downstairs buzzer. They knew that if it were drug deals the stream of people would be way more frequent. But why all those sunglasses in the middle of the night. Something was clearly up. Because it was rarely just one night but a flurry of nights and then nothing for many months or even years, it would slip out of people's consciousness until the next time. Except for a very occasional raising of voices in languages reflecting a wide range of nationalities, no one suspected anything. A visit by Robert Mugabe, which only was revealed 80 years after his death, set in motion events that eventually led to the overthrow of his government. Controversial celebrity diplomat Henry Kissinger was always ready for late night negotiations and would take center stage no matter who else was there.

*

Who's the One Speaking

In Shulamith's unpublished novel *The Adventures of Faygi and Jude in Amerika*, Jude wrote short brilliant meditations, essays as well as an occasional broadside. Even though I didn't always understand what they were about, they were definitely infused with much of the same type of genius that Shulamith's brought to her theoretical/analytic work. Now are these the words of the character? Do they reflect Shulamith's own thoughts as if she were writing about the same subject? Or is the character saying something very different than she would. Since I barely understood what was being written about I can't be sure.

In our novel *The Dreamer and the Agent* Myrna Nieves and I write about Aurora whose dreams are known to people across the globe. Aurora along with being a world class dreamer is an extraordinary poet and her dreams are evoked with breathtaking literary power. If I wrote a story by myself about a dreamer and an agent I would have to just write with enough skill to suggest Aurora's brilliance. I could never create a beautiful multilayered, multidimensional dream onto itself. For example I might say Aurora's latest dream about falling into a snowbank in Alaska where she finally finds true love went viral among her legion of admirers.

Myrna's descriptions of her own dreams just dazzle. As do her evocations of Aurora's dreams. So in our book Aurora's dreams, all written by Myrna, are stand alone literary masterpieces. As for the agent, I did write up Max's dreams. One that I actually had and a couple I totally made up.

In my long short story "In the Audience," Maxwell Berman, absolutely no relationship to Max, "was not able to write a book or produce a body of work. He didn't even try. He was the poor student who had either been broken by the system or had somehow managed to cut himself free from its socialization and was brilliant and daring.

His essays were usually very short, condensed, and often beautiful. They were small meditations. To Maxwell they seem alternately slight and deep. He wrote them only occasionally. There were long periods of inertia."

Inside the story he did just that. I could do worse than have people assume that his thoughts and journal entries are the same as my own. But they're not.

Good to know.

*

Degrees of Separation

David Baldwin, James's brother, told Gary that he Gary would be the first person after David that Jimmy would call when he came to New York. When Baldwin died it would never have even passed through anyone's mind that Gary would be asked to speak at his funeral. The official public person with human dimensions was the person being eulogized.

*

When Muriel died I wasn't asked to speak at her memorial service. Now many people loved her, and at the memorial service except for her niece, spectacular in her own right, only professional colleagues spoke. At the time it just registered as a fleeting disappointment. Writing about it I feel more hurt than I realized even five seconds ago. The memorial service was very moving. An extraordinary video of her life was shown, Her public accomplishments, again with personal dimensions, were highlighted. I learned things I hadn't known before. But the spaces in between were nowhere to be seen.

Many of our worlds are so separate that when someone dies we don't know how to get in touch with important people in their life or even know who they are. My friend Mark of over 60 years who lives in Somerville, MA just sent me a list of people to contact if something happened to him. I recognized only two names on the list.

I often went with Muriel to different doctors the last few years of her life. Sometimes we went to a hospital in Manhattan. Other times we took the Path to Newark and once there, a bus to the hospital. Cancer treatments, checkups, tests, consultations. Other times to a hospital on Long Island. One time I was waiting in the wrong place for her, I had no cell phone, adding another layer of serious anxiety to her as she waited first one place then at the train station for me to show up, which I never did. I had to make serious amends. But she did forgive me much sooner than I forgave myself.

Another time as she drove us to the Long Island hospital, we spoke about her new book project. In fact it was a book about Long Island she had already done some research on. She told me things she had uncovered. I felt so identified with her project I can't remember if I had one time suggested to her years before to write about Long Island or the moment she first told me about doing the book, it made such instant sense that I thought maybe I had suggested it. One thing was certain all her great talents, including her ability to look into the years growing up there, would be poured into the book. The information she had already unearthed in her research was straight out riveting.

I waited for her in the cafeteria for about forty minutes. When she came back her first words were, "I won't be writing my book." The doctor told her she only had a few months left to live.

*

One holiday I was invited to dinner at my friend Susie's apartment. A short time before, a wonderful documentary about her father, *Paul Goodman Changed my Life*, had been released. People at the dinner were talking about the movie. Sometime later, Susie wrote an essay about her father. Beautifully written, serious, in some ways painful, in other ways celebratory, she presented a complex picture of Paul, their relationship and the social/political environment they lived inside of.

My friend Omar, someone who worked in the restaurant in the storefront of my building, and who started renting a room in Susie's apartment a few blocks away, was also at the dinner. He and I were the only two there who knew he was related to Emile Griffith the former five time world champion boxer who also had a documentary *Ring of Fire: The Emile Griffith Story* made of his life. Omar said he would invite me to join him at Emile's annual day after Thanksgiving dinner.

Emile, whose health was precarious to begin with, grew quite ill soon thereafter and the next dinner never happened.

I watched Emile box when I was a kid. He was gorgeous, quick and strong and determined. The one fight that marked his life was the one in which he killed Benny "Kid" Paret in a welterweight championship bout. They had fought twice before, and Paret in the fights leading to this one suffered severe beatings.

March 24, 1962. It was the first or second night of Passover. I snuck off the seder table a couple of times to turn on the TV in my room to see how the fight was going. The last time only to see Benny Paret lying unconscious in the ring. He would die a number of days later. All the boxers—including Emile—that I admired and followed as a kid died horrible deaths. Omar told me he himself had once thought of being a boxer but had [I thought fortunately] hurt his shoulder in a way that prevented him from becoming one.

What was downplayed or totally hidden for a long time was what happened before the fight. There were accounts of bad feelings and serious tension at the weigh-in, but not what it was about. Paret and Griffith knew each other from their neighborhood. They had played basketball together. But at the weigh-in Paret mocked Griffith calling him a *maricón* (faggot). Griffith had to be restrained from going after Paret right there at the weigh-in.

In round 12 of a scheduled 15 round bout, Griffith landed a punch that rocked Paret. It was followed by an avalanche of punches delivered with unhinged fury. Among many things, the movie focused very intently on Griffith's sexual life, how he saw himself as bi-sexual and the struggles of being a closeted bi-sexual man in the virulently homophobic world of professional boxing as well as the larger world outside. The documentary discussed the impact of the fight on his life and the lasting impact on those closest to Benny Paret. A powerful moment of reconciliation between Emile and Paret's son is documented with great tenderness.

Years later after walking out of a gay bar he was savagely assaulted by a group of men. He was in the hospital for four months and never fully recovered from the beating.

Looking over the arc of his life, Emile said, "I kill a man and most people forgive me.... I love a man and many say I am an evil person."

The documentary about Paul Goodman also focused sharply on his bi-sexuality. The impact on his life. The impact of Paul's life on the filmmaker. As well as far ranging discussions of his political analytical work, his literary accomplishments and his role in the massive sociopolitical movements of the period.

At one point in the film a very familiar voice, one I just couldn't place, a voice deep and resonant, infusing words with profound meaning spoke about alienation and the absurd horrifying ways in which people were being socialized into a soul deadening society. It was Martin Luther King speaking about Growing Up Absurd. Not knowing who it was to influence my response, allowed me to take in the words more fully. The surprise of it and then the realization it was King was straight out exhilarating.

I didn't know Paul. I knew people who were close to him, others who had been influenced by him. Like with many things his impact on me was from a remove.

I more or less learned about what he had to say through others. And there were, as usual, differing interpretations and different versions of it. Some people took on his mannerisms and his voice patterns. At its worst they mimicked and internalized a know it all, wise, folksy, world weary, undercutting, super erudite arrogance. This mixed with Paul's actual deep creative insight, serious public engagement, moral and intellectual courage created at times a confusing and disturbing mix.

Arnie at the time had been very influenced by him. And of the people I knew, Arnie's version, or maybe more accurately, how Arnie incorporated it into his own separate transcendent prophetic vision, played an important role in the evolution of my own thinking.

"Two degrees of separation" was a common term used with varying degrees of frequency during different periods of Robert's life. The thought at the time even before social media became totally all encompassing was that everyone was connected in some way. The local grocer (the seller of vegetables, fruit and over the counter medication in what was known as a bodega or local deli or neighborhood grocery store) for example might know someone, maybe a customer, who knew someone who could connect you to a powerful or famous person or a long lost friend or relative.

It was a time of extreme atomization and loneliness. So it has been theorized that "two degrees of separation" was a compensatory notion that materialized to help offset the extreme desolation people were experiencing at the time. Whether real or illusory people took the notion in as both playful and comforting.

People now agree that the ascension of what was known as social media and the decades right before it, were the precursor to The Ice Age of Frozen Emotions that descended in the late 21st Century and lasted for almost a hundred years before what was then optimistically labeled The Great Thaw began. As we all know too well, and there is no need to go into it here, it turned out much differently than that.

In distant hindsight everything seems clear. Everything but what the consequences would have been if the road not taken had been taken.

*

My neighbor traveling on Virgin Airlines saw me in a short video about places to go in New York. It was a close-up of me sitting at a table in a cafe in the Village drinking coffee and writing. Another time a friend and I were sitting in Washington Sq Park when someone approached us and very politely asked if he could take our photo. I felt flattered and was more than open to it. My friend grew all huffy and lectured him about invading our space, or whatever term was used at the time. So that was it. Hadn't felt put upon at all. Just disappointed as he turned and left without taking our picture.

Another time I was sitting at a table by the window of a cafe. Maybe even the same one in the Virgin Airline ad. A man smiling from the street warmly gestured towards his camera asking through that gesture if he could take my photo. I nodded. He came in, silently took my photo and lightly touched my cheek as he left.

The iconic painting **Poet sitting in Cafe Window** *was inspired by a photo very likely of Robert which when it first appeared on a poster for an exhibit was a sensation in its own right. The painting also has been spoofed countless times. Most pointedly and famously in* **Branding,** *a critically acclaimed series of cartoons about the commodification of the arts.*

Being Written About

Lee Cronbach, composer, itinerant musician, playing the organ at a church during Sunday morning services in the Philippines where he went to retire with his lover of many years who was from the Philippines. His memoir still being written when he died, hilarious, screwball, soulful, totally unpredictable. Jumping with off the wall description of people and events. The varied groups he played music with, the most memorable performing with the legendary Cockettes a gay drag group in the 1970s. He was about to write about his fraught very negative experiences in academia before he died. In 2009 he released his album Angel Dreams shortly after Arnie's death. He dedicated the title song Angel Dreams, one of the most beautiful songs I have ever heard, to Arnie and Coltrane. In the liner notes Lee wrote very warmly about Arnie and his impact on the world. We played Angel Dreams at Arnie's memorial event a few months later. And his family played it at Lee's own funeral in 2024.

I sent Lee some photos of Arnie, Charlotte Hastings and myself from the 1970s. I met him in Berkeley in 1964. I was beyond curious what Lee would write.

*

Stanley Aronowitz: For example, two of my friends, Robert Roth and Arnie Sachar, publish an occasional journal of fiction, poetry, and politics, *And Then*, whose costs are defrayed by the editors and some of their friends. Robert distributes one of the NYU newspapers around Washington Square Park and Arnie lives on what remains of a modest inheritance. Both are always on the edge but seem to keep their balance. [The End of Bohemia]

*

ROB ROGUE

by Paul Meyers

Rob Rogue moved to West 10th Street.
The literary scene was hardly complete.

He got together immortal Pens about town.
Untold Authors and James Baldwin found.

And, New Yorkers, then –
grew the magazine *And Then*!

It was born on a historic night,
to render New York with inside light.

Soon the world was chiming,
pieces from many lands arriving

Poems from the Caribbean,
Germany, England and Argentina.

Bound by moments midst ages.
Voices chanted on hallowed Pages.

Ballads for beloved ones gone.
Nocturnal shadows by black swans.

Shelley sealed them between cloth.
In the orb of a spiral court.

Rob and Arnie would aspire
to paper a home with written fire.

Rob Rogue!
Famed beyond fashion or vogue.

Rob the renowned. Rob the bold.
Rob Rogue! Rob Rogue!

Near the end of part one of Carletta's memoir she mentions my name. We haven't yet met but it foreshadows our friendship to come.

I make a cameo appearance in *Hands Up Herbie!* the graphic biography by Joey Perr about his father Herb Perr that Joey released a few years ago. I feel very flattered by that. And very proud of it. As does *And Then* in which Joey, Herb, Joey's sister Rosa, and Joey's mother Mimi have all appeared in over the years. There is also a reproduction of a piece by Joey when he was 8. It was a combination of words and images published in *And Then*. It was the first page of that issue. All this adds to my fierce attachment to the book. An attachment I first felt when Herb told me with great excitement about the project that he and Joey had embarked on a few years before his death.

Irving Wexler appears very often in *Hands Up Herbie!* He and Herb were incredibly close friends who collaborated on major projects over the years.

Carletta called me this morning to mark Arnie's birthday. Arnie died 15 years ago (had accidentally typed " tears ago").

Recently Marguerite Bunyan told me she came across an essay by Arnie in an early issue of *And Then* that she said spoke with such prescient insight about the hell we have descended into. She sent the issue of the magazine to a friend to read. Said also she wrote a poem that morning inspired by Arnie's piece which she dedicated to him.

A character loosely based on me appears as a supporting actor in Irving's short story masterpiece *Will the Morning Be Any Kinder Than the Night*. I remember next to nothing about that character. More importantly the story was inspired by Arnie. The situations described were mostly fictional. And his description of the character would not be what he would have written if he was describing the real Arnie. But he catches his fearfulness, his awkwardness and his genius. Arnie was very easily recognizable. Paul McIsaac read the whole story on WBAI where Arnie had a following as a caller and occasional guest. People meeting him, or hearing his voice in a room, would light up and say how eloquent and brilliant his calls were. The same is true of Carletta whose years at WBAI as a broadcaster captured the imagination of thousands upon thousands of listeners.

Arnie was both embarrassed and flattered by Irving's story. He also felt in some ways seriously stigmatized by it. Yet the surge of warmth of people's response to the story was also very much part of the mix in how he responded to it.

Irving wrote it with great love. In some sense embracing Arnie's stigma holding it close to his heart. He also wrote a story based on a love affair, again fiction, with a woman with a serious disability. She was furious and felt exploited. Wasn't terribly impressed by the tenderness of the description or the love he felt for her writing it. He removed the story from his soon to be published collection of short stories.

*

There are diaries and journals, works of fiction, essays, poetry, book reviews, videos of that period discovered in various archives, in abandoned warehouses. One archeological dig unearthed steel vaults containing well preserved written journals, diaries as well as valuable digital artifacts.

This brings me to a somewhat awkward place.

As I have often written Robert has been depicted as a visionary poet as well as a shy somewhat clueless heartthrob. However it has recently been asserted that newly uncovered evidence shows that Robert was instrumental in creating this perception of himself. Until now that perception has withstood the test of time. Obviously the definitions of sex, desire and magnetism have changed over time. But no matter how fluid the definitions it never seemed to make any difference. I want to be clear I am not making light about how things have changed or minimize the importance of the ways sex, desire and magnetism has been transformed into whole other ways of roystering, known at that time as "connecting." This is clearly well worth pursuing.

But back to the controversy. The theory goes that Robert who was not known for his guile, had in fact perfected an aura of charismatic innocence that he continually used to his advantage. It was a manipulative ruse, allowing him to plant subliminal messages, known as fantasy manipulation, to be discovered at future intervals. Each discovery, accompanied by great fanfare, would be thought of as an exciting new discovery. But in fact it was calculated to scramble historic accuracy. So what would feel like breathtaking discoveries that further burnished his reputation, were really deftly placed subliminal messages planted for future discovery. He is now seen by many as a savvy image manipulator rather than the sexy humble heartthrob that inspired countless love ballads.

A vocal minority is actively pushing back. They call this "cynical revisionist history" designed to complicate matters and cast derision on someone who embodies a vital counter model to a retro cynicism emerging everywhere you look. They indignantly insist that there is no subterfuge involved. There is absolutely no reason to doubt that he was what he always has been presented as.

So many mysteries still left unanswered. I don't know what to believe.

Arnold Sachar, known only as Arnie, a shadow presence through the ages, was a philosopher, poet, social critic and prophet. Known for his intense focus, rare eloquence, serious cultural analysis there are very few recordings of him speaking. So his reputation is based on people's retelling.

Over the centuries people would only need to close their eyes and conjure up his eloquence. The cadences, the intense focus, the moral intensity. The insight into alienation, societal anguish and the profound social struggles of the era constantly being updated in people's imagination. But again very unusual for that period there are precious few recordings of any kind of him speaking. So his reputation and accounts of his great oratory skills have been passed on through the ages void of concrete examples of it.

At a recent gathering at the School of Prophetic Adaptation ten scholars presented their version of how they imagined Arnie would have responded to the present.

A hushed silence would come over a room whenever Arnie gathered himself to speak. It is a powerful tradition now for a room to grow absolutely silent as each presenter is about to talk.

In markedly individual voices each speaker entered a state of profound poetic eloquence. As I mentioned above but it bears repeating, in an era where everything was recorded there are no more than a few snippets of Arnie speaking. Yet when people talk about the great orators through History, Arnie's name is always high among them.

****

Airless Spaces

> bullet: *Contempt is always unjustified. Wait and see*—Shulamith Firestone [*And Then* 4, 1992]

In early 2025 Shulamith's book *Airless Spaces* first published in 1998 was reissued by Semiotext[e] the original publisher and a few weeks later by Silver Press located in the UK.

> "This book comes out of a long, lonely adventure. A season in hell. The result is a series of devastating observations made entirely without rhetoric. It operates like a parable—deceptively simple and stark, almost imagistic as little pieces fit together with little pieces pretending to be about small outcast lives when in fact it is an encyclopedia of our age—a harrowing record of what really goes on among us where the wounds of life bring on the invasions of institutions, which inflict still more suffering—a stifling atmosphere of isolations where souls are automatically and indelibly lost. This is a prophetic book with enormous consequences since airless spaces multiply and begin to take over." — Kate Millet

The book has been getting much more media attention this time around than when it first came out. Long comprehensive book reviews. At times weird settling of scores with opaque accounts of ancient conflicts. Whole bunch of comments about her life. A life in the telling that is frozen in two time frames. When she was a young incandescent radical feminist theorist who ignited the second wave of the women's liberation movement. And much later as a ravaged broken impoverished woman in the grip of mental illness. There were discussions of the state and fate of the women's movement, lessons learned, lessons not learned, lessons unlearned. Descriptions of where the writers themselves are now in relationship to their younger selves. There is often a recycling from one piece to the next of information as established fact that simply never happened. But now has become part of the official story of her life. A particularly painful example of this is the repeated story of Shulamith's sister Laya Firestone Seghi coming to New York and seeing her panhandling in the street. Whether this was true of Shulamith or not, it was not something she ever saw.

The culture machine asserting itself in unconscious but revealing ways. Whether you're visible or invisible you are a captive of it.

Chris Kraus in her intro to the U.S. edition of *Airless Spaces* wrote "Firestone didn't publish any more books until *Airless Spaces* came out in 1998." A statement repeated many times in other works written about her. The implication being that what? That she hadn't been writing in all that time. Or for that matter she hadn't written anything after *Airless Spaces* that was published. Or that something only exists as real if it has been published. It is in the self-interest of publishers, even serious small publishers like Semiotext[e] to help create that illusion, though clearly never to be stated as such. No one seemed curious enough to find out in fact what she may have been doing.

Since I don't think you need to "produce" to in any way justify your life, I feel put into a bind. Still in Shulamith's case she wrote at least two novels which I read that haven't gotten published. One which seems to have disappeared entirely. Also she submitted a manuscript of over a hundred poems to literary agent Francis Golden rightly known for representing serious radical and progressive writers only to have Golden decline to represent her. The same thing happened with Carletta who sent a novel to Golden. Thinking they already knew and understood what was being written did not allow them to fully read and appreciate the works, saying in essence there was nothing new or original about them.

Needing to project themselves as more than just gatekeepers of the culture machine, more than mere first line functionaries there to sift through material to send on to publishers, they had to come up with something negative to justify their decision as well as their role in the process. Not that "We don't think it will sell." Or "We have too many people to represent now." Or more to the point "We know what publishers are looking for and need to accommodate them or they will stop taking our calls." As much as I loved what both Carletta and Shulamith sent, I am not saying that they should have been chosen over others to represent. Nor that they should have been published over other people. That too is part of the seductive hook of the machine. Arguing over who is really worthy, who is not. Why that person not chosen was a horrible injustice. Agreeing, disagreeing, complaining, affirming, basically validating their authority to name and confer legitimacy. All the while giving you a false sense of your own power in doing so.

Of course never mentioned are the extraordinary quilts Shulamith made, some on display at her memorial service or the stunning clothing a friend of hers described, made out of scraps of material she found in the streets.

But of particular importance to me was that Shulamith appeared a number of times in *And Then* during the 1990s with prose, art work, poetry and a literary form she called bullets, which are very short meditations on far ranging subjects. Also one of the stories later appeared in *Airless Spaces*.

As much as I think I am free of what functions as the system of legitimization, I found myself hesitant to assert that. What does appearing in a small obscure publication have to do with *publishing* which is a different category altogether.

One time she made about 50 small drawings of everyday items—faucets, shoelaces, hats, chairs etc—some she called Homely Objects, others she called Beautiful Objects. She said they were party favors to be given out at the launch of the new issue of *And Then*. Where does wacky, loving, joyous community affirming creativity factor into any of this?

A year or two before *Airless Spaces* came out, Shulamith wrote an extraordinary poem "Vending in the Street" about her descent into hell. Step by step, stage by stage. It was not included in a feminist anthology about first person accounts of years in the movement and what happened afterward. I told my friend, one of the editors of the anthology, that I thought it would be a mistake not to include it. My friend was extremely defensive about it so I let it drop. Shulamith was hurt by the rejection. And as good as the anthology turned out to be, it felt very hollow at the core to me. During the time she described, I saw her sitting in the street looking deranged, a shopping bag lady surrounded by clothes and/or books. It scared me half to death. Didn't know what to do. Had to gather myself and essentially ran away.

I mentioned the poem to Lana, Shulamith's biographer who found it while going through boxes of Shulamith's things stored at Laya's house. With Laya's permission we published it in *And Then* 22.

The work of Lana Povitz the great 21st century oral historian was instrumental in me becoming an across millennia scholar. The tools we work with now are vastly different than the significantly more limited ones she had then. But learning from her to cherish any small detail, knowing the whole of everything might be contained within any one detail is something I attempt to emulate. Nothing ever got by her. Whenever I lose heart, when I get confused or hit a rough spot (a favorite term of mine from that period) or lose my edge (another favorite) she is one of the people whose work I return to keep me going.

On top of that I now learn she was friends with Robert. Nothing about that period ever surprises me.

While pouring through boxes, Lana stumbled onto *The Adventures of Faygi and Jude in Amerika* an unpublished novel by Shulamith.

Shortly before or shortly after reading Shulamith's novel, I read part one of Carletta's memoir. It was something else to read both these works in such close proximity. I read them almost as an entry.

Both works are filled with information as people continually discover things about the society and about themselves. There is some overlap in terms of places written about and actual real people who pop into both. We see movements as they form, and the life and struggles within them. We see the class, racial, gender interactions of people who in serious and significant ways are in powerful social, political, cultural movements trying to create new forms of contact and profound political/economic/social transformation. Very subtle and tender and clear eyed descriptions of people trying to work/live their way through the massive contradictions that exist—sometimes succeeding, sometimes not. Carletta's memoir is a more hopeful quest for understanding and change. Shulamith's novel is much more grim though filled with powerful descriptions of explosive intense transcendent moments of contact.

While I am still here, what about that lost novel? When Shulamith asked me to read it she said it was an absolutely accurate account of what it was like when that was the universe she inhabited. If only in that way it would be an invaluable and rare account from someone living inside of that world. It was a world made up of a family of master spies. I don't remember how many there were but not too many. They were constantly donning different masks, dramatically changing whatever outfits/disguises they were wearing. A world filled with never ending intrigue and deception. It was impossible to keep up with the ever swirling spinning frantic changes. One friend when visiting her in the hospital said Shulamith touched her face and remarked that she was wearing a mask.

Shortly after the U.S. edition of *Airless Spaces* came out, Silver Press sent her sister Laya a copy of the soon to be released UK edition. Like Semiotext[e] their edition had two prominent feminists, political radicals, Lola Olufemi and Hannah Proctor, in this case writers from the UK, writing the introduction and the afterword. This in an attempt to bring attention to the book and help introduce people, particularly a new generation of young women to Shulamith's work. They asked Laya for her blessing.

There was one big problem though.

Excerpts from emails Laya sent to Sarah Shin publisher of Silver Press:

> "Further, regarding *Airless Spaces*, [Shulamith] wrote to Jim Fleming (founding editor at Autonomedia, publisher of Semiotext(e) books at that time) about her photograph on the back, 'I think I need it here because there will be no preface or anything in the book itself to explain it or me to the browsers... I am still waiting for a copy of my contract which should state that I have some say in the cover design, along with other things discussed over the phone.'"

> "In a letter to Chris Kraus, she contemplated writing a brief (page or so) introduction basically saying 'that the deadpan of both narrative content and style is intentional. But I hope that is self-evident and I don't care for sociological explanations of fiction. Better yet is not to worry and to simply frame the shorts with lots of space around them, as in poetry.'"

A couple of years later in discussing how she wanted the re-issuing of *The Dialectic of Sex* to be presented she wrote:

> "I am not really in favor of altering the context of the book in this manner...I might consider it if it were the work of a radical theorist I admire, such as T-Grace Atkinson's *Amazon Odyssey* or some of the work of Ellen Willis. But

> I prefer the *Modern Library* approach: each book standing alone on its own merits, together constituting a rich feminist resource."
>
> "From this and more, we can see how much thought Shulamith gave to her work's presentation. She consistently wanted as little interference as possible between her words and her readers' experience of them."

Sarah had known nothing about how Shulamith wanted her book presented. She wanted to do right by Shulamith as well as the writers the press had commissioned. She was dogged in trying to see if a solution could be found. She and Laya, both vulnerable, open, serious, had a series of remarkable back and forths trying to find a solution.

And they did.

Part one of the book would be *Airless Spaces* presented exactly how Shulamith would have wanted it to be. No commentary before or after. Part two sharply separated from part one would be The Shulamith Firestone Reader. It would include Lola Olufemi, Hannah Proctor, Chris Kraus who wrote the intro for the Semiotext[e] edition, Susan Faludi whose 2013 essay in the New Yorker about Shulamith was used as the afterword, something by Laya, and a piece by Lourdes Cintron who had been Shulamith's Intensive Case Manager and to whom *Airless Spaces* was dedicated. In form, focus and content six very different pieces.

Lori Hiris who I first met through Carletta and then years later met again through Shulamith took the photo of Shulamith that appeared on the covers of both the Semiotext[e] and Silver Press editions.

Early one morning over twenty-five years ago Lori and I shot baskets in a schoolyard in Greenwich Village. Shulamith, who had come with Lori, sat with her back against the fence taking it all in.

****

Pete Wilson

Excerpt from *Health Proxy*:

> Pete eventually began to live a more private existence. He felt safer out of the snake pit of social movements. He was bitter about how he had been treated. But he did not like where he wound up. He felt forced out of public life where he could be, in his own particularly methodical and precise way, wildly creative. Being a private person was not a choice he made easily. And it was not something he liked being.
>
> Over the years when people wanted to interview him about his public role, about the early period of the gay liberation movement or about his social and political ideas, he would refuse. Even when the intention of the interviewer was sincere, he felt his opinions and accounts would be distorted. This I think grew in part out of a certain preciousness. But in truth he was very careful in his thoughts, very raw in his explorations, very vulnerable and truthful.
>
> He was also thin-skinned. It is hard, maybe even impossible, to understand another person. Pete often was misrepresented. At times maliciously. Often not. But to understand him you had to listen and try not to interpret what he said from any preconceptions you might have. It was easy to misunderstand him. The upshot of this was that people stopped writing about him. He would rather have been written out of history than have had his thoughts misrepresented. This invisibility was another source of disappointment as well as some bitterness. It was a

double-bind he had found himself in and he created a double-bind for himself in how he responded.

Two Photos

There is a photo of me when I was about 25. It was taken by my good friend Pat Dagler, a wonderful photographer who died very young from a horrible illness. She was a black woman with enormous charm, passion, and deep personal/political commitments. I loved her dearly. I don't know what has happened to her amazing collection of photos.

I remember very vividly when the photo was taken. It was during a softball game in Central Park in 1969. There's a baseball glove on my lap and I think I am eating a flower. What struck me most about the photo when I first saw it was how sexy and alive I looked, at least to myself, when in actuality I felt worn out and beyond depressed when it was taken. I had hit rock bottom.

Pat gave me two other photos she took that day. One was of my girlfriend Charlotte Hastings. Her face glowing with a smile that lit up the universe. The other photo was of me and Charlotte embracing, with Arnie walking on a small hill in the background carrying his briefcase. The game was organized by another friend, Peter Wolff. All are dead now.

Another photo was taken about 15 years ago when I was in my mid 60s. The great photographer George Malave asked if he could come over to photograph me. It was for a project he was working on. For the next couple of hours he shot me from various angles and from various locations in my apartment. Nothing came out right. I sensed his frustration. But maybe it was more mine than his. I hated how I looked in every one of the photos he took. Something drastic needed to be done. Suddenly I flashed on my downstairs neighbor, a strikingly beautiful, very thin, very dark woman from Zimbabwe. Someone in her late 20s or early 30s with real flair and charisma. Imagining myself being her, I put on a wide brimmed black hat that had a small red heart pinned on it and sat on a chair in the hallway. The very next photo was the one that he would use. Most striking to me was that I looked much,

much younger than I had in any of the other photos. So much so I was embarrassed that people would think the photo had been touched up. Still, I seriously doubt anyone looking at it would see a breathtaking Zimbabwean beauty. But that is exactly who I see whenever I look at it.

Another photo was taken by Bill Cofone for the cover of my book *Book of Pieces*. Hours of photos in the hot sun until one just jumped out. He actually sold it at an exhibit of his work to someone who never met me. Similarly a photo taken when I was in my late 30s by Marguerite Bunyan where I look dreamy, sexy, soulful. Way before the internet I gave copies of it to a few friends. A friend of my friend Regina, again someone I never met, asked for a copy, framed it and put it on her wall.

I acted in a few student movies as a favor for a friend. In one wearing an apron and chef's hat and performing in front of an imagined studio audience, I baked maybe the most extraordinary chocolate cake ever. The video went viral.

In another film, not a student film, *The Village Rain Garden* I played a cutthroat developer with some real villainous lines. Unfortunately the movie was never released.

In a one hour long movie *Tom, Sally and the Marquis DeSade* directed by George Spencer I was the Marquis de Sade in part one and Thomas Jefferson in part two. The movie was filmed during the last painful horrible, at times glorious year, of my mother's life. No matter how depressed, exhausted, depleted I was, no matter how deep my pain and panic, I straight out lit up the screen. If I looked in the mirror a second before the filming or a second after, I looked haggard worn pale, nothing like I did on the screen.

I had a bit role in two feature films where my friend Marvin Schwartz was the star. Marvin became an actor at 59 and he brought the same off the wall genius to his roles as he did to his extraordinary career as a photographer. In both movies he played a serial killer.

No role is ever too small not to have a major impact. In *I Hate You!* I am down by the river off in the shadows tying my shoes getting ready for a run. The serial killer spotted me. First ignoring me, then realizing how isolated we were, circled back and killed me. I was his 13th victim. It turned out to be one murder too many. At the screening as I was attacked the audience howled in laughter. The director was surprised but very adaptable, and reedited the movie turning it from a murder thriller into a murder comedy.

In the second film *New York Blood* my character had informed on someone resulting in a long prison sentence. After the guy was released he went on a killing spree. But I was his primary target. He finally tracked me down, tortured me for hours and then murdered me. As the scene was filmed [in my apartment], make-up was periodically re-applied to show the effects of the torture. So evocative was the scene that I actually screamed out in terror when I saw it in the theater. Afterward on their way out of the theater members of the audience complimented me on my performance. Originally I had a different role. I was an on call doctor for a brothel. In one scene I was having sex with two women there. The doctor though was dropped from the movie, replaced by the snitch who was more crucial to the story. I tried to get a copy of the sex scene but it was nowhere to be found.

A quick detour. Many, many decades ago I was a voice over for a sexist dolphin in a cartoon that a friend created. I even sang a song which took some doing. The audience booed each time I appeared. It was shown in many alternative film festivals.

This as I said was long ago, very long ago. But it's definitely fun remembering the boos but also remembering the slight twinge of wanting to say, even though no one knew I was in the audience, that really is the dolphin speaking not me.

Two friends, Ian Vollmer who I first met that day, and Dyske Suematsu were thinking of doing a series of documentaries about people who were pursuing their passions. Something I hadn't conceptualized myself as doing, still don't, but was fine being seen that way. It was filmed in my apartment with close-ups on books strewn about, various photos focused in on, and dust everywhere.

Dyske is a writer of great ability to examine serious and complex political/cultural/psychologic issues, often shedding light on things that at best I had been only dimly aware of. He is also a food maven who travels far and wide throughout the city. I always enjoy wherever we end up when we go out to eat. He also has been central to the production of recent issues of *And Then*.

As for Ian, he once came to my mother's apartment near the end of her life to see if he could interview her. The film equipment frightened her. He came again a short time later, now a few weeks after her death and interviewed me in her living room. I had grown a beard during this period of mourning, shocking me with how white it was. He opened up space for me to reflect very deeply on her life and its impact on me. I am forever grateful to him for this.

Years later he took a beautiful photo of a much older me for the cover of my book *No End in Sight*.

We also collaborated in making a mini video masterpiece *Perfume*. Hendrik van Oordt composed the music, Lotte van den Dikkenberg-Methorst played the piano, I wrote the words, and Ian brilliantly directed and filmed Alejandra Mandelblum performing a breathtaking gender fluid interpretation of the words and music.

Alejandra also did the cover art for *No End in Sight*.

More recently Carletta interviewed me for my 81st birthday. Adjusting again to my very older self, I do like how I look. It is something to be interviewed by such a close friend who is one of the most eloquent, insightful, expansive and perceptive people on the planet. Someone who I have now worked with for decades both on the magazine and countless other projects.

And just yesterday visiting my friend Arlene King she showed me stunning photos from one of the small gatherings with different friends that I had during my 60th birthday year.

*

From my early twenties until even now I have been confused with different celebrities and public figures. Not that I look like them but that I am them. I have been confused for rock stars, classical musicians, tennis players, writers, movement leaders, track stars, actors. Many of whom I had never heard of.

Eyes following me as I enter restaurants, waiters asking for autographs for a customer across the room, timid fans, particularity when I was younger, following me in the street for blocks on end working up the nerve to talk to me, being approached on subways, once at a wedding someone spoke with great admiration of my work, at times hearing a name I don't recognize being whispered as I enter a room.

[One seriously unpleasant exception. A man with dead vacant eyes approached me on a street adjacent to Washington Square Park and threatened me if I didn't come to the park that night and pay him what I owed him on a drug deal. He looked like he could kill me without even an ounce of remorse if he learned afterward I was not the guy he was looking for.]

I once attended three one act plays. Two women independent of each other came over to me in the lobby immediately afterwards to say how great I was in the first play. The actor I was confused with was at least 30 years younger, much huskier and taller than me, clean shaven with a full head of slicked back black hair. My hair was half gone and the rest mostly gray/white with a touch of brown. I hadn't shaved for a week. I learned over the years that it was useless to deny being the person I was confused for so I just thanked them.

A few years ago, twice in one week people said if they didn't know he was dead, they would be sure I was Léo Ferré someone I had never heard of. After the second person mentioned it I looked him up. He looked more like me than I did.

Léo was a Monégasque poet, composer, and singer. He was born two years before my mother. There were real overlaps between his politics and mine. He was a mesmerizing performer.

Such a powerful voice and such presence. Since we looked so much alike, I decided to study how he held his body, how he projected his voice, how he interacted with the audience. The next couple of readings I put what I learned to good use. I projected my voice in ways I rarely had before, exuded confidence, and connected strongly with the audience.

At a third reading I forgot everything I had learned. Somewhere midway I could hear the drone of my voice and remembered Léo. My shoulders suddenly straightened themselves, my voice became sharper, clearer more present. The audience perked up and fed its energy back to me.

The pandemic killed all that. I am again more tentative and less secure. Recently at Zoom protest poetry events I have been able to submit short video collaborations I did with Hendrik van Oordt, Lotte van den Dikkenberg-Methorst and different guest artists instead.

Collaborations (in addition to ones I have already written about)

FREDY RONCALLA AND ROBERT ROTH

"Our next one is supposed to be about food.
What do you know about food?"
"You're supposed to eat it."

I love collaborating with people on projects and writing and other types of things.

Your energies merging, the knowledge and perspective and talent of the other person(s) bringing dimensions to what you are [writing about, working on, thinking about], dimensions I clearly don't have. Or helping surface talents, ideas, thoughts, feelings, even knowledge that I do have and was unaware of.

One great thing about collaborations is I can celebrate what we've done, brag about it in ways different than something I've done only by myself. Because it involves other people and not to do so diminishes their achievement.

Transatlanticism written through emails with Danish musician, artist, writer Jens Magnussen. A multi year back and forth epic poem of over 300 pages (not including six months worth of pages lost due to some technical glitch that while no doubt brilliant, no one but us would know that anything was missing. And we ourselves have no memory of what was in there).

Lennox Raphael, originally from Trinidad who I became close friends with in the 1960s when he was living in New York and who

Jens became best friends with in Denmark decades later when he permanently moved there, came up with the title. He also wrote the introduction. Adding an extra magical dimension to the whole.

Lennox died a couple of years later devastating us both.

Early on Jens and I would respond the same day or at the very worst within a day or two. Later on, there could be long gaps between responses. You would ride with what was immediately written before. So you were constantly shifting direction and winding up somewhere maybe very different from where you thought you were heading.

When I stayed with Jens in his apartment in Copenhagen he felt we were in too close proximity, so we suspended writing our poem while I was there.

By the end I couldn't tell what stanzas Jens wrote and what stanzas I wrote. Occasionally you could by the spelling, for example in one stanza it might be "color" in another "colour." We basically didn't change anything except if there was an obvious error. There were so many twists and turns involving a cast of thousands that we didn't keep track. Any mistakes or inconsistencies along those lines that we discovered later we just kept in there.

One time, for a month, I just assumed, as we exchanged stanzas, that our story during that early period was taking place in Copenhagen. Everything I wrote therefore would have that in mind: only to find out Jens assumed everything was taking place in Brooklyn. Neither of us having said anything explicitly until he referred to Brooklyn in one of his stanzas. I then had to make the adjustment that we had been in Brooklyn all along.

Another time I introduced a character who was Egyptian in her mid 20s and a feature writer for *The New York Times*. Her name was Salwa, the same name as a young Egyptian woman I knew, except that the Salwa I knew, so vibrantly alive with a hysterical sense of humor, was a bit younger than this imagined Salwa; the Salwa in our story somewhat different, but still with more than a bit of the other Salwa in her; but Jens assumed Salwa was a man's name. How would he know Salwa was a very common women's name in Egypt? Since she was so vividly a woman in my head I just assumed it was self-evidently so on the page; but at one point Jens wrote "he," so Salwa instantly became a man. I had then to immediately and totally reconfigure the character in my head. The new Salwa then became an Egyptian man in his 40s, still a writer for the *Times*, but in a more senior role: someone who was working through an increasingly fraught relationship to his job, also now becoming the uncle of another character, Dalia, a young Parisian Muslim teenager whose song *The Diaspora is Everywhere, Everywhere is the Diaspora* was sweeping the globe. I love this Dalia about as much as I can love anyone; her grit, her passion, her poetic genius; her role in our poem such a compelling one: a lot of drama; a lot of pain; a lot of joy; lots of chaos. A lot of everything.

I met a woman from Egypt and told her the story of Salwa and how to me (as opposed to Jens) she instantly transitioned in the poem from being a woman to a man. She laughed and said, "All of your Egyptian readers will be constantly confused when they read your book."

When we started, there were many self-contained stanzas with rich poetic intensity, short incidents described, short meditations, occasionally a few pages of a story and then onto something else. The first hundred pages or so were quite dense. If anyone could get through those pages (I told people if they felt bogged down they should skip ahead) the rest would flow out into much longer stories. And then finally a very long intergalactic epic drama. That is how I wound up writing science fiction by being continually pulled along by Jens' genius and imagination. Whenever I made any effort to get out of that world, feeling I had reached my limit, Jens would write something that roped me back into the story.

****

I met Hendrik van Oordt in Amsterdam while visiting my family there. He was extremely intense and generous in his attention. We kept in touch by email. At some point he asked if I would like to collaborate with him. He would compose a piece and I would write words. Quite often I have asked different friends to write the words with me. Maybe 1 to 5 lines (which on rare occasions have extended into more lines). Artwork would also be included. The pieces would be posted on YouTube. None have exceeded five minutes. Most have been far shorter. We have done more than 170 of them so far. This includes a number of videos using Hendrik's music and my words. The different artists and video artists have done extraordinarily beautiful work. Somehow all the different elements seem to play almost magically off each other. Generally it is Hendrik who comes up with an idea. Occasionally I do. There are times I take an idea of his and run with it in a direction far from what he had expected. Once in a while there is a push pull as we need to accommodate the other's sense of what is being attempted. It is an interesting process to give up something that you like but that doesn't work in the larger creation. Hendrik is also a writer and a visual artist. His compositions for our project are short, all very different, yet distinct. People talk glowingly about his music to me. The visual artists who have participated have come from many places around the globe. Our creations have been very different from each other. Sometimes playful, sometimes mournful, sometimes overtly political, sometimes meditative and deep. The great pianist Lotte van den Dikkenberg-Methorst performs in almost every one. Here and there a guest musician performs instead. For the most part Hendrik brings all the elements together. It is always mind blowing seeing them for the first time. The video artists who have used his music and my words have created mini masterpieces with them.

Early on, I felt I was piggybacking on the pure talent and hard work of Hendrik, Lotte (who has developed a significant following among my friends) and all the artists involved. To compose music, to perform it, to create art, to direct a video took hours of time and focus. After doing so many I feel I am a proud equal partner in the process.

Hendrik: Robert is too modest! All his texts stand as good poetry in their own right. It is stand-alone art that just happens to combine well with my music and the images contributed by other artists. The only merit I have is that I started the whole thing, because I felt that too many artists sit alone in their corner and that collaboration can spark the artistic fire and that we need more art if we are to keep civilization alive. And although I cannot speak for Robert, I guess he has a similar drive, as reflected in his magazine, *And Then* ... I love Robert's lines and very original viewpoints («A lost thought is found under a sock», the text for Usual Argument with Death and many others). His contribution is equally strong to mine and for me a challenge to write for (the third pillar being the excellent artists we manage to interest and the fourth being Lotte, who plays with a lot of feeling). Being Protestants at heart, the Dutch tend not to hand out glowing accolades but a number of friends have commented on Robert's texts and find them insightful or funny or interesting. But I'm Dutch too and too much praise makes me feel uneasy, and so, here's to future work, hopefully as inspired!

I am deeply touched by what Hendrik wrote.

Arnie and I wrote public statements where we laid out as accurately and forcefully and as clearly as we could, things we were arguing for.

Of all the things they did separately or together these position papers were the most turgid, convoluted, difficult to follow, not so much because of their tangled complexity but because of the "alright already" I invariably would blurt out feeling suffocated by its compulsive monotonous tone. There is just so much of the "underneath the underneath" I can take.

Yet, somehow the statements issued into the most animated discussions and letter exchanges. Sparks flying everywhere. Robert and Arnie's own individual responses were as charged up as the others. As the saying goes, So, what do I know?

These public broadsides were different from petitions that we wrote and circulated to gather signatures for.

In writing public petitions you have to make the statement broad enough for a wide range of people to sign and yet not compromise your own basic principles. You don't want to ask someone to sign something and in the process be pushed into endorsing a secondary agenda that they might decide to overlook because they want to make a statement about a pressing problem. To put someone in that position was something we tried as much as possible to avoid doing.

One statement we wrote was in defense of the rights of Nazis marching in Skokie, Ill where many Holocaust survivors lived. Arguing in part that the freedom to speak and the freedom to listen were basic to any movement committed to liberation.

Staughton Lynd, radical historian, lawyer and political activist, wrote us a note saying that he would sign the petition. But he added he would be considerably more comfortable if we added something to the effect of, "We express our solidarity with the people of Skokie." Arnie and I initially didn't want any "sentimentality" in the statement. We were making our argument solely on "principle." Sentimentality in the service of principle, we thought, diluted the point. But fortunately that was only a tiny part of our feelings. Our statement was devoid of a certain human connectedness. Arnie and I were being too clever by a half. Staughton was right and we knew it immediately. To our credit his request chastened us. We didn't hesitate a second to add his sentence to the petition. We knew he was right.

The petition appeared in various libertarian socialist /anarchist, pacifist and anti-war publications.

Another major effort was writing a petition in the early 1980s about the sexual politics of the period. There was a sharp and bitter divide within both the gay and women's movement. Our purpose was to address what we felt was a ferocious sex negative and punitive streak driving one side of the divide.

Arnie, Marty Duberman and I worked on our statement and tried to gather signatures. If someone had reservations we tried to accommodate those reservations if it didn't undermine what we were trying to say. It was a delicate and often painstaking process. In the end we got a number of signatures.

We asked Ellen Willis if she would sign it. She had some nuanced differences with our wording which reflected actual nuanced differences with our positions. So instead she and her women's group wrote their own statement. But Ellen didn't want to disassociate herself from our statement so she suggested we submit them as an entry. Together, the two statements with their subtle but real differences echoed each other and expanded the discussion underlining the seriousness and depth of exploration we were all committed to. Ann Snitow signed both petitions forming an actual bridge between the two. Our petitions appeared in a number of publications. The two I remember were the magazine *Heresies*, and *Pleasure and Danger*, a book that emerged from the historic 1982 Barnard Sex Conference. I couldn't find my copy which is buried somewhere in my apartment. I called Carol Jochnowitz who I knew had a copy. I wanted to find a copy of the two petitions in order to reproduce them here. So people would see specifically what they were stating.

It has been over 40 years since the book came out and Carol, one of the most profound social thinkers of any era, remembered the cover in vivid detail. "An image of a woman in high heels standing at the foot of a stairway going up into suggestive darkness, and by her feet an overnight case. A lovely assemblage of symbols of transgression and liberation." Her book also was buried somewhere on her shelf but she had no idea where.

I found a PDF of the book and our petition was not there. But there was another petition which Arnie and I had signed along with a huge number of other people defending the conference from assaults directed against it.

Making my task infinitely harder, Robert by his own admission was very good at pointing in the direction of something relevant but not all that good at accurately describing what would be found there. So I wouldn't call them dead ends exactly.

I am starting to complain about everything. I am having a hard time of it. Too many things that would take forever to explain are going wrong with my life. I think I am starting to bring the frustrations of my life into my research. I'm getting more irritated by things Robert is doing. I am beginning to think everything he ever did, he did just to irritate me.

In addition to "Leslie Klein's Petition," Arnie and I wrote "The Tower of Babel," maybe our most important work. It was a poem made up of clashing slogans, chants, incantations from all sides of the Middle East horror show. The slogans, positions, incantations kept flying out, crashing against each other with ever increasing speed and intensity. It could have been written today. In fact a number of people have said that to me recently. Some of the slogans had significantly more truth than others. Some in fact represented our own positions and thoughts about it. But together they formed a horrible dehumanizing din that drowned everything else out.

From *No End in Sight*:

In helping me with my written work, Pete [Wilson]was like a master jeweler who could put that one extra cut in a stone that would turn a rock into a rare gem. Yes, I do feel that about the work that he helped me complete.

A good editor merges with the writer, and here I'm talking about a consensual relationship where there is no coercion to make a change. The editor enters into the consciousness of the writer, merges with it. It's a strange relationship. It is a collaboration, a deep collaboration where the role of the editor can be both minimized or exaggerated.

I've returned the favor to other people. Parts of me, not just the parts of the other person that I helped bring out, are embedded in the works of many friends. Just like dimensions of Pete and other friends are embedded in my work.

My short story "In the Audience," the piece Pete helped me the most with, is a good study in the intricacies of the dynamic.

It was a long short story. It had the feel of a novella, even a novel. It was about people who inhabited an alternative universe of radicals, who had one foot in and one foot out of the mainstream world that they were trying to change, overthrow and yet find a place in.

I would come to Pete when I finished a draft of a section. He would look at it, make the sentences more precise. He would introduce more refined elements to the thoughts. The story I was telling was absorbing. And there was much there that was pure gold. But he turned it into something else.

In the writing of one section of the story his contribution was even more basic. It was written from the vantage point of a woman. I interviewed a couple of women friends about how a woman might feel in the situation I was writing about. I took notes. I visited Pete. Told him what I was trying to get at. Told him what my friends had said. He proceeded to dictate the words of that section to me. As he was dictating I altered the words to more precisely reflect what I had in mind. I went home, wrote the whole section, incorporating what we had done that afternoon with other elements I wanted in that section and later went back to Pete who then further refined what I had done. There were five sections altogether. Only once did I reject anything Pete suggested. He was, from one angle, a junior partner in the process.

So was it a collaboration? Yes! A collaboration of equals in relation to the creation of the short story? No. To make him co-author seemed a distortion.

To make him anything less seemed inadequate. I asked Pete if he wanted to be credited as co-author. He thought that was ridiculous. And of course if he were really the co-author the story would have been quite different. He asked me if I would mind dedicating the story to him. "Look, I do have an ego," he said almost apologetically. And so that is what we settled on.

The same was true of Jim Stoller who I write about elsewhere. Over the years, before his death, Jim added dimensions to what I showed him that simply were not there before.

Notebooks

I have been pouring over recent discovered folders of random Roth fragments which without attribution also include an occasional work of a friend.

You have to immerse yourself in the weeds of various periods in his life to understand them. But of course that is exactly what drew me to his work, his life and the period(s) he lived in in the first place. I find there is some consistency that seems to exist out of time and space inside the very confines of the time and space he wrote them in. Noticeably missing are terms, words, expressions if not issues that can quickly identify the period he is writing in. But even there, so much seemed to have not fully registered on him in terms of many of the historical references, and developments, as well as cultural shifts that kept swirling around him during his lifetime. Rarely does he mention a musician other than a friend, or a writer other than a friend, or movie star other than a friend. Even in his fiction, smartphones, computers and the like rarely if ever appear. But somehow you almost unconsciously add them in some stories, while not add them in others, depending when you think the story takes place. Similarly there is the oft repeated exchange he had with a prominent radical feminist from Japan, identified only as Akemi in his writings, who with cutting irritation once chastised him by saying, "How can you call yourself a social critic when you don't pay attention to how people dress?"

From recorded interviews at the time, people would with some pleasure speak on how they helped Robert dress his characters.

The ancient adage often quoted at the time but has since long fallen out of use was, "The more things change the more they stay the same." This notion of things was both a blessing and a curse in how Robert often saw things. He would keep coming back to the same few points no matter what else was happening. This would at times issue into penetrating analysis filled with concrete vivid descriptions that captured and revealed much of the world he lived in, which is why I was so drawn to him in the first place. It seemed like a time that was pivotal, filled with passion, mystery. A lot there to discover. Other times they seemed like recycled truisms significantly devoid of their original power. I do allow for the possibility I just got weary of them. As the saying went, "Familiarity breeds contempt." That's way too harsh. But it does provide clues in fact to something I am living through right now. I feel people shunning me for reasons I can't fathom. Will my explorations of the past shed any light on what I am going through now. Does it make sense to weave it into my project?

Fortunately in contextualizing Robert's life the crucial external social political cultural realities, even if they couldn't be found in his work, were not all that hard to find. In fact they were everywhere.

Textual analysis of his writing reveals many unconscious patterns forming over time. Some seem like very deliberate shifts in his politics, or in his "take" on things. But others seem more unconscious than conscious. A melancholy taking hold, replacing sharp expressions of anguish and rage. I plan on including a glossary, a dictionary and an intricate chronicling of how language kept changing during his lifespan. Many of those changes seemed to have totally bypassed him. At least in the works so far discovered.

Selections From Recently Discovered Later Roth Fragments

Every horror revealed is only as real as the function it serves

My friend had a framed magazine cover that had a multicolored brilliantly done caricature of Winston Churchill that focused in on his imperial lust as well as his stone hearted willingness to sacrifice British soldiers and all of India in pursuit of it. It was very sharp and clever. The colors jumped right off the page. It felt liberating to see. It stripped a vile racist, imperial figure bare of all pretenses and revealed a deep ugliness in Churchill and the British empire. Then one day I looked more closely at it. I saw the date buried deep within the design and realized it was the cover of a satirical magazine published in Nazi

Germany during the war. It was Nazi propaganda totally and brilliantly on target.

I hesitated, then mentioned it to my friend who obviously had no idea that was the case. The next time I visited I saw he had taken it down.

I was on my way to Riverside Church to celebrate the 50th anniversary of the founding of Boricua College as well as its 48th graduation ceremony. While walking I was thinking, more obsessing about a column about "woke" in the *New York Times* I had read that morning and the range of comments from readers that responded. I remembered an experience many decades before at this very same historic church. I think it was a weekend conference on homelessness. I attended a session by William Sloan Coffin, a Christian minister deeply involved in the civil rights and peace movements. It was a Sunday morning and he made a joke, just a throw away line really, about what it took to get so many people to attend church on a Sunday morning.

I certainly didn't love it. But even William Coffin could be nervous and say something foolish. In another context it would be an affectionate warm playful comment. But here it stung. Though that seems too strong a word. Stung slightly maybe is more accurate. Or not.

I am not Christian. And I am neither religious nor not religious. Even saying that declares something that feels off. It was a small thing obviously. And as a joke it fell totally flat in the room. But I still remember it. So it cut deeper than I might like to admit. And more so now.

I remember after my father died my mother brought my brother and me to an ultra orthodox Jewish hotel somewhere in the country to celebrate the first two days of Passover. We were cut off from the outside world. No TV, no radio, no cars coming in or out. The second day fell on a Sunday and my mother said in passing that it was Easter. I hadn't known it. I hadn't realized the liberation in not knowing it.

The moment my mother mentioned it I felt the oppressive weight of being a Jew in Christian America sweep over me. It was only in the not knowing that I experienced what being free of it could feel like. When I lived in a neighborhood that was quite dangerous I didn't know how much fear was a part of me until I crossed over to another far less dangerous neighborhood and experienced the fear instantly lifting.

*

Language keeps shifting, keeps changing, keeps adapting, recycling, inverting, shedding light on, obscuring, revealing, imprisoning, liberating. Things change, are in flux, stay the same. I don't remember what word was used before "the homeless" came into the language to describe the huge increase, explosion, or just the increased visibility of people driven into the streets, into shelters. People living out of their cars, whole families living out of vans. People moving back to their families, crashing on couches of friends. I don't remember what people living in those conditions were called before.

Homeless Homelessness was a potent social political category that responded to a huge exploding crisis. Or possibly the increased visibility of a severe problem that was already there. I remember the first time I heard it, it felt also like there was an edge of paternalistic concern laced with pity attached to it.

The far larger feeling was gratefulness that a powerful new category had been created to speak about a massive social political systemic crime. I had no words available and had not fully, or even marginally conceptualized it in the way it needed to be addressed. This new category shed serious light on a massive problem. It had a sweep and breath and urgency to it.

Recently the term "unhoused" has surfaced as a word preferable to "homeless." It has sort of, kind of, so far partially, taken hold. Many people use them interchangeably. Many people are not aware of the new term at all. Is there a significant difference between the two? I once heard but don't remember what the distinction was. Which doesn't make it any less or more important.

In the meantime the harsh economic assault intensifies. More poverty, more desperation. More desolation.

Recently "unsheltered" was a new term I heard.

*

Just this morning I was writing about how my own writing has lost much of its vitality and originality. Unlike when I was younger, I have too many categories and words at my disposal. Rather than having to come up with something to more fully express things I think and feel, I say to myself, "Why brother. That is good enough."

I worked as a writing tutor at a local college. I very much avoided interjecting my own political/social opinions into the sessions. Other than it being a requirement of the job I very much didn't want to do it independent of that. One day I inadvertently violated this very serious commitment on my part. A young woman from South Korea was writing an essay about Gay Marriage. She used the term "same sex touch." I found it so evocative and beautiful. I said what an extraordinarily beautiful way to describe it. She said, "No, I'm arguing against it." I apologized profusely and we both started laughing. At the end of the session, I said, "Forgive me, I am really sorry but I still think that is such a beautiful way to describe it. Do you mind if I one day use it myself?" She said "Sure" and started laughing again.

*

Despair. Loneliness. Are crucial things that need to be addressed. Not pandered to. One commenter to the *New York Times*, to use an extreme example, wrote with great urgency about eliminating birthright citizenship as if it didn't end today the world would come apart tomorrow. How did it become an issue of such desperate, my life depends on it immediacy. Since I am an anarchist, pacifist, sex radical among many other categories that confine me, define and certainly aren't the whole of me I am pretty much on the outside of many of these discussions.

There might be maybe 500 people in the country that roughly think similarly to me. I don't represent much of a demographic. I have no idea what strategies will work or not work to win an election. Or more importantly what would be needed to build a movement. The thing with strategies is deciding what issues will be brought front and center, what will be muted or even discarded. Who will be further marginalized, ignored for the "greater good." Who will be abandoned. Who will be betrayed.

*

Always balancing false choices where some choices are far worse than others. Things keep spinning in all directions at once. But perpetual states of pondering false choices becomes a prison unto itself.

One of the great if limited results of the Bernie Sanders campaign was bringing serious if somewhat watered down ideas into the mainstream and winning some important victories and gaining some concessions. As well as igniting people's imagination that something infinitely better is possible. The downside is that it gave a false hope and sense of what actually could be accomplished by working within the system. Rationalizations start to set in.

To protect real as well as imagined gains, accommodations are made, each one making some sense, that keep diluting and at times significantly betraying the goals you are working towards.

During the 2024 presidential campaign the progressive wing of the Democratic party downplayed the war on Gaza, for example. Not changing their words exactly, which were serious but limited in the first place, just the frequency and intensity with which they were spoken.

Turning an extreme emergency into a box to be checked, but not focused on.

*

People talking about alienation and despair, crucial concerns in my own social/political/cultural understanding, for some reason stops at the water's edge.

James Baldwin once said, "Do I really want to be integrated into a burning house?" One major thread running through the early liberation movements in the 1960s and 70s, was to look at the deep psychic forms of repression and terror (fear of freedom) that issued into acceptance and shoring up as well as the desire for the oppressive structure we were living under.

Somehow attempts to address the deep terrors that issue into various forms of oppression—economic, sexual, racial, ecological, psychological—have been reduced to "cultural" issues, ceding the full potency of what is at stake to others to use them for their own nefarious purposes.

Conservatives seizing on the increase in fentanyl deaths, focus on isolation, alienation, loneliness, desperation. They speak about the economic misery in formerly flourishing industrial sections of the country. Offering nothing more than a red hot pan to jump back into the fire from, they keep working towards imposing multiple forms of repression, economic exploitation, social control, sexual and psychic repression and soul deadening spirit crushing alienated forms of community.

The US creates the despair, the pain, the oppression, the false high of "family, community, religion" the bitter reality of exploitation, repression, psychic misery, the crushing of hope, and drug cartels are there to provide poisonous relief.

This has been a recurring theme in Robert's work. First suggested, though not explicitly articulated, in his late teens. His essays then focused on social and economic injustice, racism and assaults on free speech. It was in his poetry and fiction that personal and societal sadness, sexual longing and repression were first written about. The inclusion of social psychology as a basic feature of his social political writings are traced to meeting Arnie Sachar in the early 1960s. Arnie was considered a brilliant orator, who infused his social criticism with a deep focus on repression and alienation. He was particularly well known for his intensive research and brilliant analysis of the social psychological roots of war fever.

In Robert's ground breaking short story, "In the Audience," a group of radicals—socialists, anarchists, sex radicals, feminists, gay activists—with one foot in and one foot out of the dominant culture, try to navigate the contradictions in their lives. One character, loosely based on Robert, though he denied it whenever asked, makes dramatic and bold pronouncements that, independent of his protestations, echo many of his own thoughts. But without the usual endless qualifications.

From a scene taking place in a Yoga class:

> Contemplation, silence, community, a dark sexuality are at the core of Maxwell's social vision.
>
> Fear of death and of life freeze the body and the spirit. Destruction, war machines, grinding social injustice, brutal nation states grow out of this terror. And the social structures take on a life and history of their own, and constrict human and social possibilities even further. In Yoga, as in absorbing conversation, or in an intense sexual encounter, one briefly is able to glimpse a state different from what is. It is terrifying and often not very clear. But one has stepped outside everyday experience and consciousness. Things can be different. And even if only that has become clear, something significant and dangerous has taken place.

*

Here a Bomb, There a Bomb
Everywhere a Boom Boom

US bomb
Israel bomb
Russia bomb
Syria bomb

Iran bomb
Ukraine bomb
Pakistan bomb
French bomb
China bomb
Hamas bomb
Hezbollah bomb
Saudi Arabia bomb

Hey, you forgot India

India bomb
Turkey bomb
Venezuela bomb
Iraq bomb
Japan bomb
Egypt bomb
German bomb
UK bomb
Australia bomb
Philippine bomb
Sudan bomb

Here a bomb, there a bomb
Ho Hum another bomb
Everywhere a boom boom

Houthie bomb
Taiwan bomb
N Korea bomb
S Korea bomb

Righteous bomb
Revenge bomb
Resistance bomb
Retaliation bomb
Rationalization bomb

Oops!
Wrong place dropped on bomb

Here a bomb, there a bomb
Everywhere a boom boom
Everywhere a kill kill
Everywhere DEATH DEATH

*

To demonize a demon is a way to justify one's own hideous crimes.

Sohnya Sayres spoke to me about war logic. How one thing leads to another to another. How one justification creates another and then on to another. All the while making sense out of murderous nonsense.

Blood lust, power lust, greed are among the most lethal and addictive drugs in the world.

Genocide, ethnic cleansing, crimes against humanity.

Proportionality, war crimes, rules of engagement. Collateral damage, Violation of international law. Armed resistance is permitted against an occupying power.

What is legal what is not. A just war fought illegally. An illegal war fought within the bounds of what would be permitted if it were a just war. International court of justice.

A hundred people blown up in one village is tragic collateral damage. In the next a war crime.

Weapons of Mass destruction. No option is off the table.

Intricate, refined at times pathological distinctions inside specific legal definitions. And each one by speaking of what is forbidden allows for horrors that are permitted. Very decent people have set up these legal systems in an attempt to put some constraint on the most heinous forms of violence. Even these fragile constraints are under severe attack now.

*

The colloquial meaning of words like genocide, crimes against humanity, ethnic cleansing seem far more accurate than their legal definitions.

*

This year marked the 80th anniversary commemorating the dropping of the atomic bombs on Hiroshima and Nagasaki. Rather than it being a time of serious self-reflection, some defenders of Israel's war on Gaza, as well as other wars, keep pointing to it as what was necessary to defeat Nazi Germany and Imperial Japan. That in the face of an evil so monstrous, the Nazis in particular are always the ones pointed to, overwhelming lethal force leading to unconditional surrender was the only moral choice to make. Since then one enemy after another has been compared to the Nazis. One leader after another is said to be worse than Hitler.

In a comment in the Times, a commenter named Raisinet wrote, "It just doesn't make sense to compare Israel's flattening of Gaza, a small territory under Israel's control, to the allied bombings of Germany, from which one of the most aggressive industrialized armies was literally attempting to take over the world."

The fire bombing and destruction of the German city of Dresden in World War ll, where huge numbers of citizens were burned to death, is cited as further proof that in any fight against enemies as monstrous as the Nazis almost anything is justified. For some though, no matter what else has happened, no matter whatever other horrors and crimes they advocate for, the sight of starving children in Gaza has been an "optic" that even they recoil from.

But others keep doubling and tripling down. Carnage in search of a justification has been their calling card. Over and over again they keep looking for their next fix. When one war ends, then onto the next.

One columnist who is never fazed by any of it, keeps arguing that creating famine is one of his favorite, most effective weapons of war while lamenting bitterly about it being categorized as a war crime. In some ways underlining the absurdity of why one thing is a war crime while another isn't. Yet also underscoring the added degree of cynicism and depravity of those who operate under almost no constraints.

*

Hamas massacring 1200 people in southern Israel on October 7, 2023. Also in a calculated act of dehumanization and torture, took 251 hostages, many of whom subsequently died, to be used as bargaining chips in future negotiations. Which included the release of a much larger number of Palestinians held in Israeli prisons, often under awful conditions and few if any legal protections.

Hamas, part resistance movement, part severely repressive theocratic sex hating, freedom hating, brutal regime. Supplied with sophisticated weapons by Iran, a regional power.

Iran an oppressive theocratic state that imposes extreme repression on its population. Like Biden did with Ukraine, they parcel out weapons to their proxies, just enough to do their bidding yet still not enough to allow the types of autonomous action which they fear would jeopardize whatever larger designs they have. In going on its murderous rampage Hamas defied the constrictions placed on it by its powerful [benefactor, arms supplier, ally, regional master].

How do you talk about Hamas and Iran, soul crushing theocratic regimes, without feeding the [gruesome, ghoulish] propaganda apparatus of Israel and the US to justify the mass murder committed in Gaza and the increasing violence against Palestinians on the West Bank, and the bombing of Iran.

How to be in solidarity with people—this extends to many other situations as well—who face treacherous, violent repression from their own government, while simultaneously facing a ruthless external enemy whose greed, power lust, bloodlust, whose need to control and vanquish is never sated.

*

Julian Beck, anarchist, pacifist, cofounder of The Living Theatre, spent his life putting himself in harm's way physically, emotionally, psychologically, resisting militarism, economic injustice and the soul crushing death culture. He was beaten up, arrested, driven out of the country. The War on Vietnam was in full throttle. He was on a TV show and was asked what the NLF (The National Liberation Front) should do to resist. His voice, dramatic, filled with emotion, responded, "The NLF should surrender now." It was startling. If I said it it might have had some poetic resonance. He saying it had profound moral force. When he said the NLF should surrender now, he wasn't talking about the Vietnamese capitulating to domination, terror and imperial aggression. He imagined massive non-violent, deeply creative, forms of resistance. [From my book *No End in Sight.*]

On the eve of the Russian invasion I heard a Ukrainian pacifist, socialist calling for something similar. He had no illusions of the forces that were about to be unleashed. Nor of the manipulations and ploys by all involved that led up to it. He wanted a resistance similar to the one Beck had called for. He was at that point resigned and mournful that Zelensky had chosen the "war machine option" instead. I have no idea of whatever happened to him since.

*

Among the many pieces here and there scattered in Robert's notebooks were things clearly and not so clearly written by others. Robert often quoted other people in his work. Since he knew who wrote what, he was very random and inconsistent in identifying work he saved. I spent much time trying to identify who those writers were.

Here for example, I am almost certain, was something written by his friend Bernie Tuchman. While roughly similar in perspective, there are subtle differences in focus, analysis and language that seem very consistent with other works written by Bernie. In a section devoted entirely to him, Ferris Wheels and Roller Coasters, *I go into a deeper analysis about his writing and his life. I start from when he was a boy, both alienated and insatiably curious, in colorful iconic Coney Island, New York. With its world famous amusement park and bustling beach and boardwalk, it was a magnet for tourists, thrill seekers, revelers, families and roaming teenagers. It was also the home of many first and second generation immigrants and people relocating from elsewhere in the country. It was located in the borough of Brooklyn, a vibrant city within a city that has no contemporary counterpart. I then trace Bernie's evolution as an economist, socialist, political activist and poet. At this time, I don't know if the following in particular was ever used by Robert. It is just meant as an example of the types of things he would save and use to enhance something he was writing about:*

> Which side are you on? Neither! The architecture of oppression always needs an outside enemy to justify

> compelled internal unity. The task of those seeking liberation is more difficult. Liberation for "us" but not for "them" leads precisely to the Messianic mindset which prefigures endless war. We may not be able to achieve universalist goals, but we must have them as our guiding principle, seeking solidarity on that basis across boundaries which have been constructed by narrower visions, and which keep us fighting each other.

And this:

> The unifying secular humanist principle is a bias towards equality of life prospects. It is a world in which the grandchildren of people already alive are not motivated by a toxic need for revenge, nor fear of revenge.

More from Robert's notebooks. This from one labeled SHORT TAKES.

As I get older, and then much older, and older still I feel an ominous future bearing down on me.

> Five doctors in eight days
> As body parts I never knew existed
> Keep making themselves known to me

I was at a party and the great libertarian socialist Joanne Landy asked me to dance. Within a second she asked me what I thought of the equally great Daniel Singer's most recent article in The Nation. I don't remember my answer. But I have never forgotten and have always cherished the question.

*

I once wound up in a room of therapists discussing what they did. One said she was a movement therapist. I thought, what an extraordinary thing to be. I wonder what that entails. I am very slow on the uptake. It took awhile to realize she wasn't talking about left or progressive or radical political movements, but using physical movement as part of her therapy. Interesting in its own right. But still...

*

My friend Amber, the name she wrote under, a great poet and a mainstay of the Living Theatre had over many years written poems about vegetables, a couple of which have always been confused for fruits. Her poems appeared in many underground publications and were just bursting with color, taste, information and often enough profound social analysis. You never knew what vegetable would be written about next. Or when. And no vegetable was ever seen as unworthy to be written about. We had spoken about preparing a feast, a pot luck of vegetables to accompany a reading of her work. Sadly she died before that happened.

*

At my local cafe each time you buy a coffee they stamp a card. After 10 you are entitled the next time to get a free drink. I lost the card that would entitle me to that drink. So I started again with a new card. After ten I put it on the counter and got my free drink. While drinking it a worker came over to me and gave me my card back. I put it in my wallet and later realized that I could use it to get another free drink. Is it ethical to use this card as a substitute to the one I lost. I always leave a large tip when I get my free coffee.

*

I was sitting on a stoop in Greenwich Village with a fashion designer from Zimbabwe. As we watched people walk by she gave me a master class in jeans. The cost of the different jeans, the material they were made of, the different ways they looked (they all looked the same to me) and what the person was trying to convey about themselves by the jeans they were wearing. And who would likely pick up on it. A couple of decades earlier, this time I was with a radical feminist from Japan who was not terribly impressed with my obliviousness about clothing. With real irritation she said, "How can you call yourself a social critic if you don't pay attention to how people are dressed?" Why do I always keep coming back to this memory?

*

I often have to translate a word into another word in my mind. And the emotional and intellectual resonance of the previous word still attaches itself to the change. So it is somewhat forced and willed. For example I always and still don't know what word to use Hispanic, Latino, Latina and now Latinx. Whenever I use one word as opposed to another I wince slightly.

In my book *No End in Sight*, on a whole range of things, my solution was to list different possibilities in brackets so the reader could choose which word to use or more accurately offer the subtle but maybe real differences that each word conveys. At times revealing the [prejudice, bigotry, received wisdom] it was attempting to address.

*

From the time of my birth "Oh what a beautiful baby," until now at 81 I have had a beauty that I have had to keep under wraps, with various degrees of success, because at its most intense people would faint in its presence. I have made it very clear in my will that my secret(s) will be revealed no sooner than 75 years after my death.

*

Irv Noren, an outstanding major league outfielder in the 1950s and a captivating story teller, was being interviewed in 2017 after having been voted into the Jamestown, NY Hall of Fame. He told the story of his young daughter coming in from the outside who, when seeing Yankee teammate Mickey Mantle sitting in the living room visiting her father, started shooting daggers in his direction. Irv said, "Dear, that's Mick, Why are you looking at him like that?" Still fuming she said, "Tommy said I needed to give him seven of you [baseball cards] for one of him." Mantle started laughing and said as she was going back outside, "You should make the deal." The day before the interview Irv's daughter called and said make sure to say that Mickey was right. "I would be rich now if I had listened to him."

Cabin in Maine

If you know him as well as I do, if you have lived with him as long as I have, I found a poem by his mother written in Hungarian—authenticated by scholars at the Institute of Reality Studies—about his life as an infant and her feelings about being a young mother. So I feel I've known him from a very young age. It used to be frustrating whenever I had to read in between the lines to more fully grasp what he was thinking about. But once you know those in-between lines are really not all that different from each other, things grew much less complicated and easier to understand.

Which brings me to a little known hiatus in Robert's well ordered, oh stop it—there was nothing well ordered about it. More precisely in a life marked by long periods of inertia, stasis and dreary routine that was not even a routine, he defied all expectations when he went on a three-month retreat to a cabin in Maine with an only in case of an emergency communication contraption that his good friend Dave Neiditch, the dynamic chemical engineer known for his innovative brilliance in taking everyday discarded items and finding solutions to problems others were totally stumped by, had set up for him. Other than going for groceries every other week, he would have no human contact.

He planned on telling just a handful of people he was going away. The numbers though did keep increasing before he left. He once went away for a weekend without telling anyone and whole groups of people went into panic mode. "No I haven't heard from him." "Me neither. I tried to call. No answer." "I emailed him, I texted him, no response." He didn't want to put people through that again. If a weekend could cause all that panic what would three months away do. Yet he didn't want to have to explain himself and be subjected to everyone's responses and advice. I haven't yet discovered how he in fact did inform people.

Robert went to Maine to see if he could look into the pain he caused others. Once he entered his 80s, he was having an increasing number of quick, split-second flashes at all hours of the day and night of the pain he caused other people.

Rather than quickly force it out of consciousness, he would fully let the pain sweep over him, stay with it, live with it, and see where it would take him. The realization he came to is that to guard against being overwhelmed by the intensity of a primal pain he would lash out at others. It felt like emotional survival. Only then did he begin to understand the impact that it had on others.

There is no direct evidence about any of this, though it is vaguely alluded to in a series of poems he wrote. Also I deduced this from other writings found in what I am reasonably certain are his notebooks. Mostly from what looks to the uneducated eye like frantic scribbles, I knew it had to be rife with meaning. I was able to get access to the most advanced handwriting deciphering apparatus that is particularly effective in deciphering handwritten scrawls from that long ago era.

Many of the people he thought about were already dead, others he had no idea where they were living or even if they were still alive. As for people he was in contact with, he was genuinely afraid of how they would respond if he spoke to them about it. If my readings are correct, more often than not they would say, "Don't worry about it." Or I have no memory of that happening, or occasionally a quick thank you. And once or twice, "You think this makes it any better?"

It was after this time in Maine that he wrote Knots Unwound, *by all accounts an underground classic. Unfortunately, despite a couple of new leads, I am still trying to track it down.*

Thank You

I am deeply grateful to Robert Perron, a fiction writer of great sensitivity and depth, who took it upon himself to offer to design this book and help bring it into the world.

I want to thank Eric Slater, a wonderful literary stylist, for taking one final look at the page proofs, and catching things that I had missed, many times over.

Thank you Fredy Roncalla for coming up with the title The Genius of 10th St. Once suggested, all other possible titles flew out of my mind without leaving even a trace.

I want to thank Carletta Joy Walker, Bernie Tuchman, Myrna Nieves, Sohnya Sayres, Michael Szpakowski, and Fred Kramer, who have been with me throughout.

Marguerite Bunyan, a friend for the ages, thank you for the stunning cover art. Ian Vollmer, thank you for your "hey he ain't half bad looking" photo of me.

And to our way in the future historian, biographer, sleuth, a shout out and thank you for taking such an interest in our present, your distant past, and trying to make some sense of it all.

About the Author

Robert Roth is the author of *Book of Pieces*, *Health Proxy*, *Transatlanticism: New York—Copenhagen* (written with Jens Magnussen), *No End in Sight*, and *The Dreamer and The Agent* (written with Myrna Nieves). He is co-creator of *And Then* magazine since its beginning in 1987. Over the last number of years, he has created a series of YouTube videos combining poetry, music, and visual arts with Hendrik van Oordt and Lotte van den Dikkenberg-Methorst.

www.ingramcontent.com/pod-product-compliance
Lightning Source LLC
LaVergne TN
LVHW090612110826
845146LV00001B/360

* 9 7 9 8 9 9 1 8 3 3 8 8 2 *